Confabulating
With the Cows

Wit, Whimsy, and Occasional Wisdom
from Perry County, Indiana: 1992-94

Also by Brett Alan Sanders

Author

A Bride Called Freedom
(Bilingual Edition: Spanish translation by Sebastián R.Bekes)

Translator

Awaiting the Green Morning (Bilingual Edition), by María Rosa Lojo
Passionate Nomads, by María Rosa Lojo
We Are All Whitman(Bilingual Edition), by Luis Alberto Ambroggio

Confabulating
With the Cows

Wit, Whimsy, and Occasional Wisdom
from Perry County, Indiana: 1992-94

Brett Alan Sanders

Per Bastet

Confabulating With the Cows: Wit, Whimsy, and Occasional Wisdom from Perry County, Indiana: 1992-94

Published by Per Bastet Publications LLC, P.O. Box 3023 Corydon, IN 47112

Cover art by Joy Kirchgessner

Cover Design by T. Lee Harris

ISBN 978-1-942166-32-0

Confabulate: 1. To talk casually, chat. **2.** *Psychology.* To fill in facts in one's memory with fabrications that one believes to be facts. **3.** *Literary journalism (ie., the art of writing a newspaper or magazine column).* Artfully fibbing, mixing fact and fable, pulling the reader's leg; carrying on and making music with the animal creation, whensoever and wheresoever thou pleaseth.

To my father, Richard F. Sanders
and in memory of my mother
Carole Louise Kroessman
(December 5, 1939—September 1, 2011)

And to Anita, our three children,
and the grandchildren who have since graced our lives

Confabulating
With the Cows

Wit, Whimsy, and Occasional Wisdom
from Perry County, Indiana: 1992-94

Contents:

Foreword

1992: Rural News (Correspondent)

1992: Talk of the County (Columnist)

1993: Talk of the County

1994: Talk of the County

Foreword

Perry County, if you don't already know, is located along the Ohio River in southernmost Indiana, mostly south of Interstate 64 and at roughly the midpoint between Evansville, Indiana to the west and Louisville, Kentucky to the east. My parents both grew up here, where I also spent my toddler years before being trotted off to see the bigger world at the age of four.

Dad was a country boy, raised on the floodplain around Tobinsport (a "wide spot in the road," the locals used to joke) and graduated, at some miles distance, from the fading industrial town of Cannelton's tiny high school. Mom, on the other hand, was a city girl, if Tell City has ever really qualified as such — it boasted between five and six thousand inhabitants when she graduated from high school. In any case, the community named for that legendary marksman and fabled Swiss hero, William Tell, was and still remains the county's metropolis. Attaining, at its peak, a population of almost nine thousand, it is flanked by Cannelton (the next largest) and Troy (the oldest), while roughly northward amidst the beautiful hills and valleys of Hoosier National Forest lie a smattering of smaller towns or villages.

Mom's German ancestors, having traveled from Cincinnati with the Swiss Colonization Society, were present among the aspiring city's founders in 1858. It was from there that my father took us — fresh from the Naval Academy at

Annapolis; enlisted, oddly enough, in the Air Force — to the Arizona desert, first, and then to the southern California coast, just outside of L.A. And, though afterwards I lived more years at different locations in central and south-central Indiana than anywhere else, it was from Houston, Texas that I returned, at the age of thirty-two and in the fall of 1991, to northern Perry County near the consolidated county school where I would teach Spanish and English for the next twenty years or so.

Finally, not long after the passing of the old millennium, I arrived full circle at the one-and-a-half-story redbrick house that my grandfather had designed and built more than sixty years earlier in Tell City. I remain there to this day, across 10th Street and on the diagonal from the old Franklin School where my mom first attended. She used to sleep in the upstairs bedroom with its sloped attic ceiling where I now have my study.

But when I wrote these essays for the local paper more than two decades ago, I lived out at Leopold, first in an old white farmhouse on the village square and then in a newer single-story house on the other side of State Road 37. My most immediate stylistic influences for this project were a pair of outstanding newspaper columnists: the immensely popular Joe Aaron, who wrote for the *Evansville Courier*, and the equally beloved Texan, Leon Hale, whose essays for the *Houston Chronicle* cheered me up on many an evening after a trying day at the school where I was experiencing a first-year teacher's fiery initiation.

Somewhere I read — in a blurb or introductory note to one of Hale's books, I imagine — that he, Aaron, and the more nationally renowned Russell Baker of the *New York*

Times were the three best columnists writing anywhere in the United States at the time. If my essays, in that case, only give half as much pleasure as those masters have given me, then I will count myself at least half as fortunate.

For all these years, though, until recently returning to those essays and once more taking their measure, reminding myself also of the enthusiastic if modest following they had once attracted, I supposed their day had passed and did not seriously consider collecting them in a book. But now it seems I was wrong. And since my good friends at Per Bastet Publications have seen fit to take on this selection, it even occurs to me that they might continue to make good reading not only for later generations of Perry Countians, but for a wider range of Hoosier readers and even others far and wide.

Their thematic content, after all, is universal, as is true of any literature or art of lasting value — however superficially parochial, or regional, or local. And, what's more, beginning with the first sentence of the first little report from Leopold, before the *rural news* had grown up to be the *talk of the county*, these essays had always dared to dream big enough to encompass all of that — and, of course, to sing, just like the cows in Maurice Edwards's fields.

Tell City, Indiana
June 2017

1992: Rural News
(Correspondent)

Lorca in Leopold:
Green, how we love you!

Green has been blooming out here Lear Pool way and throughout our beautiful county. This recent cold snap notwithstanding, I have heard the trees and plants in chorus with Maurice Edwards's cows out back of our yard, singing this refrain from the Spanish poet Lorca: *Verde que te quiero verde*, green how I love you green!

Really, I heard them, and perhaps my readers have, too. But enough of that. I hope no one will mind if I take a moment from my first report to introduce myself and my reasons for taking up this assignment.

I am native to the region, if not to Leopold where I now live with Anita, my wife, our school-age children Jonathan, Nadina, and Stephanie, and Patches, the homeless cat we have taken in. My maternal grandmother, Mary Kroessman, and my aunt, Gayle Strassell, still live in Tell City, where I lived until I was four. Cousin Julie (Strassell) Hauser lives hereabouts, too. My dad, Richard Sanders, grew up in Tobinsport, and his sister, Lynda Corley, still lives in Cannelton. I had visited the county often before moving back last August to accept a position teaching Spanish and English at Perry Central.

When we left Houston, Texas last August, the world was green. Back home in Indiana the world was parched and brown but full of promise for our future. We left behind an impossibly expensive and hectic lifestyle in favor of this one where everybody is family. We hope that the new promise of spring will ultimately bear fruit for all of our new friends and neighbors.

We are grateful to many of those friends and neighbors who have made us so welcome here, but in particular we must thank Kurt and Paula Cooper, who at a moment's notice provided needed shelter. They have been kind landlords and we rejoice with them in the recent birth of a new daughter, Heather.

I remember when Paula tried to direct me by phone to the place that we would be renting from her. She pointed me to a sign that supposedly said something like, "Lear Pool, 1 mile." I choked on that one, so translating she said, "Leopold," which I understood.

Anyone wishing to educate me further about any local place names, origins, or stories is urged to give me a call. I want to hear, too, about your family events and visits, your crops, anything at all, accompanied by any amusing or heartfelt tales that you might relate. I will do my best to report in a way that will inform and entertain young and old alike.

My purpose in taking this assignment, aside from informing and entertaining, is to better acquaint myself with the community and its people, so please be in touch. My readers have the advantage, after all, of knowing me before I know all of them. If you chance to see me, remind me of who you are. I may have forgotten.

"If I was their teacher. . . ."

I was asked Friday by English student and former Leopold resident Jason Sprinkle a question in two parts: first, why did I not write about him in my first report, and second, why did I write about myself.

Let it not be said that I am slow in the redressing of ills. Jason, whom I immediately perceived last fall to be more dedicated to athletics than to academics, was nevertheless a student whose good-natured ribbing and playfulness I enjoyed. I will always remember the time my littlest daughter came up the hall from the elementary school into my classroom, just moments before the final bell, and secure in her dad's benevolent presence, smilingly reproved the class for its liveliness at that moment. "If *I* was their teacher, I would tell them to shut up," she said, to which Jason replied, rising and pointing a finger at her, "I'm glad you're not my teacher!"

This remembering of Jason in reference to myself and daughter brings me to my answer to the second part of his question: the writer approaches any subject through his or her personal experience of it. I hope that the writing will engage the reader most effectively by virtue of its having first engaged me. Last week, in any case, aside from my family introduction, I did also write of some of the first people who welcomed us to Leopold. As I get out more, away from school, and as others in the community contact me with their own stories and ideas, it is only natural that readers will begin to see more of their own names and less of mine.

The names of several people do, of course, come to mind. Sometimes as we get to know each other, misunderstandings may arise, and it is my and Anita's sincerest hope that such obstacles to shared sympathy may be done away with among all honest-hearted people in our fair community. This hope is certainly appropriate to a political season, where the sentiments shared in a public forum are not always of the kindest. It is appropriate for friends and neighbors, too, who, coming from different backgrounds and experiences, will not always tend to approach things in the same way.

I remember that the first kind neighbors at our door last fall were Julius and Bessie Genet, and since Anita, due to a visual impairment, does not drive, Bessie's companionship over the following months became a vital link in her adjustment from the noisy and peopled atmosphere of Houston to the solitude and isolation of Leopold. Sometimes our city ways must strike the Genets as peculiar, as their country ways may us. We can now laugh about the day Anita started laboring in our garden and Bessie counseled from across the way that her technique was not what this experienced observer would have advised. From the typewriter where I was working at the time, it occurred to me that the shouted admonition was rather abrupt, but time showed it to be rooted in friendliness. We hope that our own gestures to all our new neighbors, the most and least well-considered of those gestures, will be viewed in the same spirit of generosity.

Otherwise, I would be remiss if in closing I did not pick up on an oversight pointed out to me, through Anita, by Jason's grandmother, Ophelia Sprinkle, another good neighbor right here by the town square. Absorbed so much in welcoming ourselves, I failed to welcome the new neighbors who came after us, Bill and Donna Wilkins of the new B&D Grocery. They are nice folks, and we look forward to their not only working but also living in our community. Godspeed to them in clearing all necessary hurdles in realizing that goal.

Kinfolk: Ties that bind

The other week while introducing myself and my family, I allowed as to how good it was being back in Perry County where everyone is family. It seems that the more I get around, the more I see that those words are true. The bonds that unite us are ever new and surprising.

Just a week ago this past Tuesday, for instance, while waiting in line for a piece of cake after Perry Central's high school award night, I was talking with Alvin and Betty Sturgeon, who were there with their son, David. The Sturgeons, I have just learned, live at the opposite corner of our town limits just behind Good Time Charlie's, where my family and I occasionally like to grab a bite. David won first place out at the school this year for a roll-top desk he made. We all wish him well as he advances to the state competition in Indianapolis on May 23.

Alvin was talking to me about family connections, anyway. It seems he knows Tom and Gayle Strassell, my uncle and aunt, from working these several years at what is now Best Chair in Tell City. He started there in 1957 when it was still Fischer Chair, he told me, and he was just out of high school. His dad, Henry, came home one day and said, "Alvin, would you like a job?" "I guess," he answered, to which his father said, "Good, because Mr. Kroessman said to bring you in with me tomorrow."

Mr. Kroessman was my great-grandfather, Emil. Hardly more than a month ago I saw him in the *News* in a 1942 picture of Kiwanis Club members in front of the flood wall. He and his son, Marion, the grandfather I remember best, headed up Fischer

Chair for a number of years. Whenever I smell the delicious scent of freshly-cut wood, I remember my grandpa, Marion, who took me down to the factory more than once and was going to take me there again the morning after his sudden death from a heart attack, in July of 1969, when I was ten.

The Sturgeons are thus connected to me by the memory of a loved one. We are all united in sundry ways like this, whether or not by blood, which reminds me of a passage from a book that I think my readers would enjoy. The book is called *The Education of Little Tree*, by Forrest Carter, and relates in simple but eloquent prose the childhood of a Cherokee boy with his grandparents during the Depression years in the Ozarks.

"Grandpa said back before his time 'kinfolks' meant any folks that you understood and had an understanding with, so it meant 'loved folks,'" Mr. Carter writes. "But people got selfish, and brought it down to mean just blood relatives; but that actually it was never meant to mean that."

In Perry County kinfolks are all of us, despite the misunderstandings and fallings-out that sometimes beset us.

In neighboring Cannelton, for instance, where my family and I went at Dogwood Festival time to listen to our friends in the band Sassy, I wandered into a barber shop and got a trim from a guy named Mouse. Seated in the other barber chair was Floyd Freeman, who I did not know but who introduced himself, with just a touch of a smile, as a member of Tell City's newly-controversial school board. "I'm the one who abstained," he said, as dryly as if he were merely observing the weather.

Well, it seems Floyd knows my dad from Cannelton High, and his wife, Deanna, who came in moments later to collect him, was my mom's, the former Carole Kroessman's, good friend from Tell City High. When Deanna realized who I was, she gave me a hug and started reciting passages from my life. Never mind politics or abstentions: all of us here are of one cloth, and it is good to be back and a part of it.

Also it was good to see Ruth Loesch's kind words, from Tobinsport, in reference to me and my dad, even if she did leave off a *t* from my name. Bret Maverick, for whom I am told I was named, only used one in his name, and an old namesake used to chide me for wasting *t*'s in mine, but I still think the second one adds an essential touch of class.

Back home in Leopold, anyway, we are enjoying this Sunday afternoon weather from our yard swing where I am composing these lines. We just said goodbye to my parents who were here to visit Mom's mother for Mother's Day. The Sturgeons have had family, too, particularly daughters Becky and Anna, who live in the county and also work at the chair factory. Some things, it seems, are destined to remain all in the family.

Southern Indiana landscapes on my mind

Anita and I were present at Mulzer's Camp last Saturday evening for a picnic honoring Jack and Patti Wellman, Curt Richey, Norman Seifres, and Gib Williams, who are retiring this year from Perry Central. There were lots of good food and pleasant company, as well as a splendid view of the Ohio. I sat there for a while just watching the river traffic and gazing at the church steeple over at Troy.

The various rivers, streams, hills, and church steeples of southern Indiana are part of the landscape my mind remembers whenever I wander away from it. Turn me loose here with a camera and I will go far and wide just to record those images. I think of the approach to Ferdinand, from north or south, and of the monastery at St. Meinrad nestled into the beautiful autumn hills and foliage. On my initial approach to Leopold from SR 37 to the west, my first hint of the town proper was St. Augustine's spire, which reached out to me as I rounded the last bend. The church thus seemed to beckon to me, who am nevertheless not a Catholic.

Others before me have felt similarly welcomed here. At the retirement party, for instance, I was chatting with Irv and Susan Rueger, whose daughter Lydia was at the Sanders house watching the kids. Irv told me quite a remarkable tale of the welcome he and his family received about ten years past when they moved to Leopold and built a house back in the woods outside of town.

It seems the neighbors must have been watching and making their plans, Irv told me in the animated style that makes even his most ordinary statement entertaining. This is the same man who last October showed up on our doorstep dressed as Elvis. "Trick or treat, baby!" he said to Anita, who under the season's spell almost fainted. I was making the Hallows Eve rounds with our children, but Irv confirms that it was he. Lydia had put him up to it, but I digress. That is another story.

Irv's neighbors had been watching his activities, anyway, and when they saw that he was ready to put his roof on, better than a dozen men showed up to lend a hand. One of them told him to go get some beer, and when he came back the roof was already in place. One of the neighbors had been roasting a pig, so there was something solid to wash down with the beer. This was hospitality that a man used to Chicago and Evansville was unaccustomed to. It calls up images of a frontier ethic that city folks may seldom experience outside of history books.

While my own family's welcoming has not involved a roof-raising, it has by no means been insubstantial. Our new friends at the Latter-day Saint church in Tell City were there to help me unload the U-Haul, some boys from out at the school came by to assist my dad and brother and me with some of the heavy appliances, and other friends had by their efforts helped to make sure there was a place to unload. Write your names in here. Neighbors from town, as they were out, would wave or pay a call, and when we were new, or later when Anita was in the hospital for a few days and then recuperating, they would come with flowers or food. All of these gestures were what the moment demanded, and in our hearts are as great as any roof-raising.

The town itself, Catholic to the core and with St. Augustine's spire at its spiritual center, has itself been an ideal place to settle down. Since Anita does not drive, she likes being so close to two general stores, the new B&D and Guillaume's Store across the square from it. Ernest and Myrt Guillaume are among the first locals we met, and they are very representative of the friendly people who are our neighbors. The fact that I was formerly a Mormon missionary in the Catholic country of Argentina, and that my family and I still worship in that non-Protestant Christian faith, has not been a matter of discord among us. On the contrary, it is by virtue of that original acquaintance with the Spanish language that I am able to serve this community, and I very much enjoyed the Mass I attended on Christmas morning and the expression of faith evident in the lives of several of my students who were there. Father Mark's words that day, referring in part to Christ's admonition that we love each other, were appropriate to the hearts of all honest people, whatever the particulars of their faith.

Finally, I cannot fail to mention that, as many of us have already heard, St. Augustine's will be at the center of a very special celebration this summer, when the church and community not only recognize their 150th anniversary, but welcome a visiting delegation from Belgium, the little country responsible for Leopold's founding. While the pages of the *News* will undoubtedly contain more precise information in coming weeks, even without my help, my readers are still encouraged to contact me with information so that my words too may serve as a reminder, as well as a source of additional perspectives on coming events. On my own I am already looking with interest at the local history, lore, and architecture, but your phone calls are always appreciated. This is your space more than mine. I write for all of us.

Exploring the old Ransom house

As I type this report, I will be seated at my desk in the little study I have carved out of Paula Cooper's rental — "the old Ransom house," as I have heard it called — just past Leopold's town square on St. Louis Street. The house, listed on page 29 of the *Perry County Interim Report*, is classified as an I-house, a vernacular construction whose name is derived from its popularity in Indiana, Illinois, and Iowa. The house is dated to approximately 1895. It has been given a "C" rating for purposes of the current survey, "contributing" as it does to the historic flavor of the whole district.

Before browsing through other people's copies of this newly published and, locally, much reviewed book (I finally made it down to the Chamber of Commerce to pick up my own), I had no idea that the street I live on had any name or identity independent of the county road that intersects our town. There were many things that I did not know, and one or two less that I still do not. The extent of our ignorance is always astounding. We can only take comfort, I think, in that we are all pretty much in the same boat. The most wise among us knows less than the most foolish thinks he knows. Our education is an eternal project.

I have begun, anyway, to learn a little more about Paula's house. What I might have called simply a white-frame house becomes more distinct, a two-story version, as it is, of the hall-and-parlor. Rather than the traditional one-room deep and two rooms wide, ours is a bit deeper. On one side, the living room adjoins a spacious dining area to the rear, which opens to the right into the kitchen. On the other side, the kitchen adjoins a hallway with doors opening into what were two large bedrooms. The second room was at some date divided into two in allowance for an indoor bathroom. It is the other half of that partition that, having formerly held two bunkbeds with Paula's two kids, now holds my desk and a couple of shelves full of books.

A stairway goes from the dining area upstairs into a series of three walk-through rooms, which circle back to the left. The landing area is now a playroom. The girls sleep in the middle room, and Jonathan in the last. For our first couple of months here, the upstairs was entirely unlivable, and like the most recent inhabitants before us, Paula Ransom included, we limited our living space to the downstairs. Paula and Kurt had planned the remodeling before we came and were kind enough to let us move in early since we had no place else to go. Jim Rogier is the man who finally did the job, allowing us to get the kids off the mattresses in our bedroom and ourselves off the sofa bed in the living room. He did wonderful work.

It is particularly when you step into the basement that the house really does look a hundred years old. The stone foundation and wooden beams are striking, as is the pantry area with its ancient shelves inviting home food storage. At the foot of the stairs is a wood-burning furnace at whose use I have strived, sometimes impatiently, to become adept. Adjoining it is the wood room from which our furnace is fed. The pantry opens through cellar doors into the back yard.

Out front is an ample porch with wooden posts and awning. I would attempt to address its style, but am afraid to reveal so much of my ignorance. When the book starts throwing out architectural words like *transom*, *sidelight*, and *cornice return*, as well as identifying titles like *Greek Revival* and *Italianate*, I have to leave the explanations to someone else. What I need is for someone more informed than I to walk me through my own house and help me to appreciate its features.

Someone who knows the house may perhaps show me a lot about it, and I would welcome the tour. I would also like to picture more completely what the house looked like in the 1890's as opposed to the 1990's. Aside from the recent interior remodeling, and the aluminum siding that graces its exterior, I could not say very much about the changes the house has undergone, though living in it as I do I find it hard to imagine that its basic integrity has been much compromised. It is the most distinctive home I have ever lived in.

Perhaps my readers with particular knowledge of other houses, barns, outbuildings, churches, or the historical people associated with them will contact me with these stories. I will be seeking them out. Also, it would be good to read the local stories that our other correspondents might share with those of us who may not know them. I mention this because of a particular interest in seeing a little something about the Frank Sanders farm out at Tobinsport, which belonged to my great-grandfather and is also listed in the book. I imagine there are about as many stories scattered throughout our reading area as there are readers.

As far as that goes, it is a pleasure to read the words from whatever source. I regret that any fellow writer, encountering my particular style, should feel even slightly intimidated by it.[1] I would rather that it be a source of new ideas and individual inspirations that we all might share. As I tell my students, the written word, like folk music, is the property of all people, not just of an elite, and anyone with the slightest desire to dabble in it should have full reign. I am ever inspired to renewed efforts toward excellence by the individual gifts and contributions of many students, friends, and fellow educators. The people at the *News*, and out here with me in the field, are among the newest of these friends. I look forward to what they can teach me. Who of us, after all, knows anything on his own account? School is not out for us as long as there is existence.

---

1   I allude to a remark, in her May 21 column, by Tobinsport correspondent Ruth Loesch: "We recently took aboard Brett (spelled with two *t*'s) Sanders, correspondent from Leopold. I find joy in reading his column, a format somewhat different from that of most of us. Must say it increases my timidity some and perhaps by comparison exposes my limited vocabulary a bit, however his recognition of the homey atmosphere and good people in our county is pleasing to us and will surely be an incentive for him to be with us for some time to come. Welcome to our group."

Gratifying reports from a reading public

I feel gratified by reports I have been hearing, directly and indirectly, of the pleasure some people are getting from my column. I gather that my readership is growing. Nothing could make a writer-teacher happier than news that, for the simple joy of reading it, folks are picking up something he has written.

Does anyone besides me ever hear the news at ten? Reading has become a lost art, we are repeatedly told, especially among youth. Imagine my delight, then, when one of my students tells me she is reading the rural news for the first time! Just think of the variety of stories my partners and I, in our individual ways, can share to keep readers like her going.

There is no substitute, after all, for enjoyment as a motivator to reading. In Texas, while suffering the world's barbs, I would always turn for resurrecting life not only to scripture but to the warm and witty columns of Leon Hale, who wrote for the *Houston Chronicle*. Those of you who have felt at home with the style of Joe Aaron, late columnist for the *Evansville Courier*, would be equally at home with Leon's style. If any reader enjoys my column half as much as I enjoyed his, I will be immensely pleased.

Maybe it is enough, for the moment, to have accomplished a couple of lesser goals. At the end of her sixth book review for the 1991-92 school year, for example, an English student scribbled a note thanking me for forcing her to find time to do one thing she loved to do but seldom did, that is to read. It helped, I suppose, that I allowed her to select a series of popular novels by V. C. Andrews, rather than the "cultured" fare that I might have chosen for her. I was more interested in how she wrote about what she read than in what she read.

Since I tended to let my students read their own selections, they could indulge me a little whenever I would mention (again!) my favorite storybook figure of all time, the Spaniard Cervantes's windmill-chasing hero, Don Quixote. I remember reading a shortened version of the tale when about fifteen, and imagining myself to be Don Quixote's alter ego. Later I read Cervantes in a full translation, and again in Spanish. Imagine my joy when one student this year, inspired by my taking it up, started reading the book on his own, and even seemed to like it!

Joy in reading is sometimes contagious, so my readers will perhaps excuse me if I spend this column trying to spread the infection. I am reminded of a college professor who always started her class by reading different children's books to us. We were a bunch of adults going into secondary, not elementary, education, so at first we thought her practice rather odd. By semester's end, though, several of us who had not liked to read before, stood up and witnessed of having even carried the torch to others. Seldom have I seen such inspiration in a School of Education classroom!

If we in the teaching profession can inspire our students to want to read, that is a good thing, but I have always looked on summer as a great moment for parents to do the same. In my family we tend to read with each other year round, but during the summer we have even been known to unplug the TV and read more. Among the treasures we have been through together is Laura Ingalls Wilder's series of "Little House" books, which is infinitely superior to the TV series and is recommended for families with children coming up on or into their elementary years. With Jonathan I have also read C. S. Lewis's "Narnia Chronicles," a bit of spiritual fantasy beginning with a wonderful book called *The Lion, the Witch, and the Wardrobe*. Aslan, the Lion, is an effective Christ-figure, yet the story entertains without preaching. The series is recommended for families with children about ten or older, though I read it to Jonathan when he was seven or eight.

For the youngest of children may I recommend particularly the rhythms of poetry? The nursery rhymes our heritage is so rich in are especially good, as are the Hoosier poems of James Whitcomb Riley, which I will always remember attached to my grandmother's affectionate voice. As a beginning reader I was equally fascinated by Dr. Seuss's playful rhymes. Ask your librarian for help in making other selections, though the repetition of a few good poems or stories that parents and children both enjoy may be enough to start a child on the path to reading. This is especially true when the reading habit is planted early.

The pinnacle of success for me was when Stephanie, newly learning to read, on a recent Saturday preferred a book to a cartoon. It is nice to see her or Nadina or Jonathan peeking ahead at the next chapter in a book we are reading together. I would like to hear of my readers' special adventures with the written word, too, and in a future column I will include some of them.

As for the next couple of weeks, I will be in Mexico, but my words will not all go with me. I will leave a couple of columns with my editors, so look for some words about the Dr. Taylor house in Leopold, as well as the James N. Ward store now run by the Guillaumes. When I return you will hear the thoughts of some Leopold youth who have traveled with me to Mexico and with Attilia Gogel to Europe. Then the Belgian visit to Leopold is upon us. I will be present, as I know many of you will be. I can hardly wait. See you there!

Life of a resident-itinerant doctor

"The most notable house in Leopold is the Dr. John Taylor House," we read in the *Perry County Interim Report*. "This 1915-16 Sears and Roebuck Catalogue house was home to Leopold's only resident physician."

Resident physician he was, living in that house from the time of its construction in the summer of 1915 until his death from pneumonia some forty-two years ago at about eighty years of age. The word "resident" by itself, however, does not do justice to the kind of physician he was. Call him a resident "itinerant" doctor, if you will. The limits to his office were not within his house's walls; he probably went to his patients as often as they to him.

"He was a country doctor," Elsie Taylor says, sitting with me recently in the house's living area. She is sitting within feet of the waiting and attending rooms where her father-in-law used to work. Patients would come here to him, she explains, but he also went "near and far" to do their doctoring and the delivering of their babies, traveling first by horse and in later years by car.

Thomas James de la Hunt, writing in 1916 about a previous inhabitant, Dr. William P. Drumb, refers to him as Leopold's first resident physician — "If resident be the correct term describing a rural practitioner whose range of patients was scarcely narrower than the circle of Father Bessonies' parishioners." Leopold's founder, French-born Augustus Bessonies, was a traveling, or itinerant, priest, a frontier "circuit rider" whose weekly schedule took him as far east as Corydon and as far southwest as Rockport. Dr. Taylor, if not covering quite so much distance, at least knew his way comfortably around the present county limits, and traveled accordingly to whichever backwoods residence might have required his service.

This is a kind of doctor that people of my generation and younger may never directly know. Dr. Taylor was not this little community's first resident physician, but he was its last. His practice is part of a romantic past that we will want to hang onto at least in our remembrance.

As I am graciously invited into the bungalow-style house that Sears and Roebuck built, I can sense the remembrance of Dr. Taylor all around. Elsie — whose remembering extends back at least to the time she and husband Burke began living in the house with his father — is sitting in a chair beside the fireplace, where "of a night" she often sits doing the stitching on a fine quilt such as the one she is now putting together. Remembering him, she points to the room, now converted to the house's fifth bedroom, where his patients used to wait. Adjoining it, now an indoor bathroom, is the small room where he had his shelves stacked full of medicines and where he saw his patients.

Following Elsie through the downstairs (upstairs are a couple more bedrooms), I go back out from the bathroom into the living area. From there to the right are two additional bedrooms. From that living room I pass through the kitchen to a covered porch out back, with its nice view of St. Augustine's in one direction, and in the other the old Leopold schoolhouse where some of her children attended. (The house is located at the corner of St. Louis and Washington Streets, right next to the B&D and across from the post office.)

Immaculate describes the whole place, house and grounds. Approaching from the front, I pass through a shiny, silver gate. The house is white, framed by brick red on the bottom around the porch and up the chimney, and green along the top below the layered roof. Inside I am immediately struck by the room's spaciousness and the immaculate wooden beams along the ceiling and roundabout. The hardwood floor, added years later, is so shiny that I imagine it as part of a Murphy's Oil TV commercial. The walls are tastefully decorated by various religious paintings, including one, over the kitchen table, of a white-bearded man at prayer over his daily bread. On a mantelpiece is a plaque that Elsie received for twelve years of service in the cafeteria out at Perry Central School, where some of her children eventually attended.

My readers and I are indebted to Elsie for allowing me to impose on her peace and quiet to ask her about the history of the house she lives in. I also appreciate Earleane Preher's generosity in lending me her copy of Mr. de la Hunt's book, *Perry County: A History*. Earleane, currently living with her husband and daughters out Mt. Pleasant way, is of another distinguished Leopold family, and it is a pleasure recently getting to know her. Her brother, Kenny, lives out back of Anita and me, and his family are all good friends of ours. Earleane is herself an obviously bright and intelligent lady who is creating new opportunities for herself after several years spent outside of the classroom. She has just passed her tests and is interviewing for admittance to the nursing program at Humana in Louisville. We are all proud of her and wish her the very best now and beyond!

Saloons, dance halls, and a town's Belgian forebears

I recently talked with Ernest Guillaume, the latest of several successive proprietors at the James N. Ward store on Indiana Street on the north side of Leopold's square. It has been Guillaume's store for thirty-three years. The man and the store itself are both repositories of a good deal of exciting history.

Any history, if told right, is exciting stuff, and Ernest has a knack for telling it. He was not shy about letting me in on some stories, either. I could probably go back and forth with him and fill a year's worth of columns without hardly trying.

"Oh, I've got something to show you," he says when I first come in. "You're the one interested in history, right?"

He disappears through a door into the adjoining residence, which faces left as you approach the back of the store. Seconds later he emerges with an old black-and-white framed photograph of the E. Yaggi Saloon and Dance Hall that had stood in Leopold before his time. The picture was delivered to him recently by Catherine Yaggi Luckett, who owns it. Look for it to be displayed at Leopold Heritage Day on June 28.

The Yaggis, known today for their bar and catering service in Cannelton, originate right here in Leopold. The two-story saloon and dance hall, Ernest tells me, used to stand at the corner of what, according to the street names as originally platted, were Caroline and St. Louis streets, a stone's throw away from either Good Time Charlie's or the post office. The way Ernest tells me is that it stood right there where Waitman "Jiggs" Haney has his garden now. One of the Haney granddaughters is tending to a fire in a rusted can out back of the house — and I can easily imagine how the building must have stood, there on Caroline Street facing east. I wish it were still there. Ernest wonders if it went down in the same cyclone that took James N. Ward's original store, but seems to recall hearing of its having burned to the ground.

However it went out, Catherine Luckett's picture has brought it back to us. The people hanging out of the second-story window seem alive to us today. In our remembering, they are.

Did you know that Guillaume's store itself once housed a saloon and dance hall? It did. Ernest told me himself. Somewhere in the intervening years between the Wards' building of it and the Guillaumes' purchasing it, the front of the store was a dance hall, and the back room was the saloon.

Didn't I tell you this place is full of history? There are things that we youngsters would never know about if we didn't read about them or hear them spoken of.

The writing and keeping of our local and family histories is so important!

In Belgium, Ernest tells me, the history of this place is written down in perhaps more detail than we have ourselves.

"You know," he says to me at one point, "I had something happen three or four years ago." He describes how Brother Rene Bouillon from St. Meinrad came in to the store one day with a guest. "Are you Mr. Ghi-YOME?" the man asked, pronouncing Guillaume in the French manner. "Well, I'm Father So-and-So," the man went on, "and I've said all my life that if I ever came to the United States, I wanted to come to Leopold, Indiana."

Why to Leopold and not New York or Chicago, Ernest wanted to know? Because over in Belgium, where this visitor hailed from, they have a detailed history of this place. Many of Leopold's settlers "came from my valley," the visitor said, proceeding to rattle off a bunch of French-sounding names — Ro-Jay for Rogier, and so forth.

"You know," Ernest says, "that man told me things about Leopold that I didn't know?"

All because of a written tradition that kept the history alive for his people. We benefit from that historical sense ourselves as we host a Belgian delegation and realize that, in large part, we are his people. I feel a part of it myself, even if only by adoption, or by virtue of having heard the stories and written about them. My own people came to Tell City with the Swiss colonizers and to Tobin Township at other times, but, German-Swiss or French-Belgian, we are all related.

When you look for the picture of the Yaggi Saloon and Dance Hall on the 28th, also look for Prosper Guillaume's old deed to some land around here, if Ernest turns it up. Prosper, Ernest's grandfather, came from Belgium at age six and went into the Union Army at sixteen, having lied about his age. Apparently he came to be General Ulysses S. Grant's personal guard, and later got a deed that was signed by President Grant himself.

Talk about history! We could go on all night.

Next week, when I am back from the jungles of the Yucatán and Attilia Gogel's group is back from Europe, look for some of our students' experiences, yes, but also Ernest's World War II stories of the jungles of the Philippines. We may only be Perry Countian, but our garden is the world.

Incidents of travel in Mexico, Europe, and Asia

I promised a report on the various travels of a few Leopold-area residents, from Ernest Guillaume's World War II adventures in the Philippine jungles to some students' more recent travels through the jungles of the Yucatán and the cities of western Europe.

Attilia Gogel's European excursion may seem the least remote, since we can trace the coming of so many of our own ancestors from those countries. This week's Belgian visit to our community reminds us of that.

I was speaking recently with Amy Bower, who from this community was accompanied on the trip by Lydia Rueger and Jill Edwards, as well as by Lydia's mom, Sue. Amy is a 1992 graduate of Perry Central and of Attilia's German classes; Lydia and Jill, also students of German, are recent survivors of my sophomore English class.

"It's really easy to see the differences between our cultures," Amy says, "but it's also interesting to see how we're similar, and how we get some of our traditions." Among the things that you see there and will not see here, she particularly mentions the "beautiful" architecture, which is so grand and old. I talk in my column of a house's being one hundred years old, but in Europe a building may date back two thousand years. There is perspective. "Things over here look small," Amy observes in light of that perspective.

Italy, which happens to be Attilia's home country, was also Amy's favorite part of a two-week tour that took in London and

Canterbury in the British Isles; Paris in France; Florence, Assisi, Rome, and Venice in Italy; and Munich, Nuremberg, and Rotenberg in Germany. In Italy the group also visited Attilia's home town, somewhere in the vicinity of Bologna.

The people were friendly, Amy says, and the food good. They ate a lot of pasta, but Attilia also knew a lot of out-of-the-way bakeries to get good buys on breads and pastries. They ate tortellini at Attilia's brother's Italian restaurant.

The food in Mexico was not bad, either, though not everyone will agree on all counts. The least successful meals to me were one hotel's efforts at United States cuisine, and among the best a buffet that included traditional Mexican combinations of beef, chicken and pork, delicious black refried beans, and more, all complete with native music and dance for entertainment. We did see some tortillas, but not the typical Tex-Mex plates that we associate with Taco Bell. We drank a lot of Coca-Cola and purified water. In the resort city of Cancún we ate at a McDonald's.

As in Europe, the people in Mexico were hospitable, "much more than I expected," says Karl Fleming, a German student who traveled with our Spanish group. Karl and sister Gena, who also accompanied us and is entering the Spanish program as a freshman this fall, are both presently of Leopold. Lesly Wilkins, the Spanish student who invited them and is, by coincidence, their aunt, currently has a Branchville address, but the Wilkinses are building near the Flemings outside of Leopold. Karl and Lesly are both juniors this fall.

It is interesting that Karl mentions before anything else the people's friendliness. Karl is himself as friendly and happy a traveler as I ever hope to encounter. Despite his lack of a Spanish-language background, he seemed at all moments to be enjoying himself. He even took it in stride when I would forget and speak Spanish to him.

The friendliness of the Mexican people is illustrated by an early incident where a group of us, at night, stumbled on a street dance and were warmly invited to participate. Lesly and boyfriend Travis Esarey, accompanied by Gena and me, took him up on the offer, and were applauded for our boldness by our fellow dancers. Later, in Cancún, the members of a Mexican rock-'n'-roll band at the Holiday Inn next door to us invited Travis to perform with them the next evening, an event at which our group was proudly present. In a village at some distance inland, the humble descendants of Maya Indians invited us into their bamboo-and-thatch huts and allowed us to eat the guava fruit from their trees. Karl especially remembers the friendliness of the people in the open-air marketplace where we could bargain for the goods that most interested us.

"I learned a lot about people," he says, "about what extremes they'll go to for you."

Above all, the students enjoyed the beach. A word of caution, though: be sure that your sunscreen is stronger than the 100°-110° Fahrenheit Yucatán sun. Mine was not, as proved by the burn I got during a brief stretch on Sunday. (We were coming home Monday, our eighth day.)

After all of this, I have said nothing of the jungles through which we waded to see various Mayan ruins, the spiritual centers of our journey for me. Let me close, anyway, with Ernest Guillaume's recollection of the jungles in a former Spanish colony, the Philippines. He was there fighting the Japanese in WWII, and since the trees covered the view of most else, he and his companions used Mt. Pinatubo, which we know from the recent eruption, as a directional point of reference. You were forbidden to light a cigarette after dark for fear of the enemy's finding you. In a rice paddy nearby, Ernest and a buddy counted twenty-six downed planes in a two-acre area, twenty-four of them being Japanese crafts. Back in the states he recently met in Tell City a boy who hails from the same valley where his old jungle headquarters was located. Small world!

"Their faith was a ship that could not be crushed"

Fresh from the sesquicentennial festivities up at St. Augustine's, I am relaxing on this pleasantly sunny and warm Sunday afternoon. The weather has cooperated splendidly for an enjoyable and enriching celebration for everyone in attendance.

The location just a couple of blocks away has made it easy for my kids to go back and forth at will and for me to roam around with my camera while Anita visits friends in Houston.

Anita would love to have been here, too, and she left me with strict instructions to keep up with her blossoming garden and to take some pictures at Heritage Day.

To make up for my lying on the beach without her at Cancún, we got her a cut-rate fare so she could lie on the beach without me at Galveston, a stop we missed when we lived out there. To get the rate, she had to stay a weekend, and this was the only weekend she could do it.

So I bought her a souvenir T-shirt and got some pictures of the Rev. Mark Gottemoeller with a couple of his horses. If I am lucky, at least one of them will turn out. Perhaps Anita will forgive me, too, for not having gotten one with the visitors from Belgium.

Speaking of Father Mark (I always like a man with a smart-looking beard), I've heard his religious homilies only twice and been struck both times by their considered intelligence. The ritual of the Mass itself may still seem unfamiliar, and thus impersonal, to an outsider to Catholicism such as me, but when Father Mark steps forward and gestures expansively to the congregation, then addressing to us some personal thoughts that are relevant to our collective mood of thanksgiving, I feel then a very welcome part of the group. That is certainly the case afterward as I commune with various people.

The essence of Father Mark's words, which are more than worthy of reporting here, is tied into the heritage of faith, courage, and sacrifice that Leopold's primarily Belgian founders left us and that we are urged to leave our own descendants.

Have we duly considered the courage our forebears had to exhibit to accomplish what they did? First, as Father Mark very eloquently explained, they had to cross the rough Atlantic in a minimum passage of fifty days, then navigate upriver to Derby from New Orleans.

Second, when they got to this heavily forested frontier, they had to clear the land of trees that may have been as big as six feet in diameter.

Third, the Catholic people with their foreign religion and customs had to encounter the persecution of backwoodsmen who pillaged the parsonage and set fire to the church. The persistent townspeople put out the fire and kept going.

All of us in this country, whether of European, Native American, or other stock, have a heritage of courage ventured and trials or persecutions suffered. My own adopted spiritual heritage of a Mormon trail to the Rocky Mountains sensitizes me to the story of Catholic trials in Perry County. We are stronger in our faiths because of what we take from the examples of our forebears.

And how did those forebears prosper in this country, Father Mark asks? By virtue of their faith. "Their faith," he says, "was a ship that could not be crushed by the storms."

And are we to just look back to their example and passively enjoy their labors' fruits? No, he answers, we must put our hand to the plow and keep on going.

Then in another hundred years, our own descendants will remember our courage. We must remember, he says, that "we too are on a journey of faith."

These individual journeys of faith are captured in much of the memorabilia that have been on display for this occasion, and on the messages in German, French, and English on the tombstones in the church's cemetery.

I copied some inscriptions at random such as this one in English: "Francis Xavier Lemaire, Born at Jamaigne, Belgium, Apr. 18, 1832, Died Nov. 1, 1909"; this one in German: "Hier ruht Christian Maier, geb. 4 Marz. 1804, gest. 12 April 1872"; and this one in English and French: "In memory of Jean Joseph Meunier, Ne en Belgique le 21(?) Sept. 1803 et est decede le 27 Jan. 1883, Jesus Marie et Joseph, Priez pour moi."

Aside from those multilingual epitaphs (incidentally, it was exciting for this foreign language teacher to hear part of the Mass in French), I was happy to see such lengthier written records as Brother Rene Bouillon's loaned account "The Family of Joseph Bouillon," and the memoir by Andrew Etienne entitled "Memories of My Life."

Speaking of putting our hand to the plow, Andrew relates on the first page of his record of a grandfather's humorous account of some oxen that refused on a hot day to do their labor until they had first rested, plow and all, shoulder deep in the cool water and mud that was their retreat.

Sometimes our work will not go forth as rapidly or gloriously as we would like, but if we are patient, it will go forth.

Companion to that patience is the modesty inherent in Andrew's own words: "This may or may not be of very much interest to anyone other than family members and people who are mentioned in this story." So seldom do we really know the measure of what in life we have dared to venture!

Paranormal communications
at St. Louis and Lafayette

In my first report from Lear Pool back in April, I mentioned some poetic recitations that I heard from the cows that were out back at the time: *Verde que te quiero verde*, green how I love you green.

It was out at school a week or two later that one of the girls spoke to me about that. What it boiled down to is that she didn't for a second believe me, but she found it very interesting reading. Very interesting, indeed.

So it occurs to me that she — even, perhaps, a couple of you — may be interested in some other, shall we say, paranormal communications I've had of late. While I wait for your more verifiable notes and phone calls, we might even pass it off as "news."

The news is that I've walked back and forth past the old hotel at St. Louis and Lafayette Streets. I've heard ghostly voices crying out to me. I have, I swear on my grandpa Marion's 1920 edition of *Child Rhymes*! That book is by our Hoosier poet James Whitcomb Riley, who after all has had credible experience with ghouls and goblins and such.

Now, I know you're saying, "He's pulling our legs again," but that's okay. They had to call me twice before I believed.

They kept whispering, though, and oh so eerily! I couldn't quite make out their words, but I could tell it was me they wanted. So I went in last Friday afternoon to investigate. I needed material for this column, after all, so I ignored the obvious dangers.

Now, I wouldn't recommend the tour to just anyone, especially kids — if I ever find mine in there, I'll tan their hides! — but what I found was interesting. In just a moment I'll get on with the narration.

For the journalistic record, first, let me refer you again to page 29 of the *Perry County Interim Report*, which, along with Elsie Taylor's house and the St. Augustine Catholic Church and Rectory, pictures this "outstanding early hotel," observing its position as "one of the county's oldest remaining inns." The wooden structure was built in the Greek Revival architectural style circa 1830 to 1850. Presently its front is overgrown with vegetation, and the whole structure is showing the ravages of time and neglect. The windows are all broken out.

Of all the buildings in Leopold proper, this is the only one with an "outstanding" rating, which according to the inventory suggests a property of "enough historic or architectural significance that it is already listed, or should be considered for listing, in the National Register of Historic Places," and thus may be of "local, state, or national significance." The other three buildings mentioned in the preceding paragraph received "notable" ratings, indicating still above average importance and possible eligibility for National Register listing.

As I come up on the hotel, now, I wonder if that's not what the ghosts are trying to tell me. "Remember this place, remember us who were here." I don't know what will become of the building or if there's anyone with the vision and wherewithal to restore it, but for the ghosts' sake let us dream, and at last remember.

I walk in the back door and find general disarray. Broken glass, drooping ceiling paper, trash and junk everywhere. As I walk in, there's a tub and a toilet. I turn right into the kitchen and left from there into a living room up front. The building is two rooms deep and four wide, the kitchen and living rooms being the largest downstairs. In one, there's a concrete stairway going down to a cellar that I'm not bold enough this time to explore. A wooden stairway, hidden away and narrow, leads up to the immense, open attic, where I suffocate in the heavy, rising heat.

Blankets and clothes hang all around in various places. Old boots inhabit the floor. I find a very empty bottle of Bond & Lillard Kentucky straight bourbon whiskey and wonder how long ago it was consumed. There are a couple of old books, a 1910 romantic novel called *The Rosary* and an eccentric, wordy 1911 religious exploration called *The Life Everlasting*. Also a class annual, from an Air Force aviation school, vintage 1944, that I will come back to in a moment. These books I will have at home with me, if anyone can legitimately lay claim to them.

Downstairs, a small fireplace extends upwards through a closed brick chimney. Out back, joined to the main building by a connecting roof, is a padlocked room that I take for a pantry. Back inside the main building, my most dramatic discovery is a couple of figures that literally jump out of the wood they are carved into. The painted colors are faded and dirty, but the bosomy woman has black hair flying in some wind and a red dress with golden sleeves. The man sports what I take as a Napoleonic hat and look, appropriate to the French-Belgian settlers to this community. I imagine that these are the ghostly personages I have been hearing. If not for that, for their belonging so much to this specific place, I am tempted to also bring them home.

The name I find in the Air Force class yearbook — *The Gremlin*, appropriately enough — appears to be no real ghost, though whether alive or dead today I can't say. Pictured among the "grads" is one Lamar P. Horton of Leopold, Indiana, his goggled and helmeted features suggesting adventures of which I know nothing. Any friend or family still in the area is welcome to the book in exchange for some of those stories.

With this, now, I leave the hotel. As I am writing these words, I feel that the spirits must be pacified, but my romantic imagination still roams over the fertile terrain of the place's past and possible future. I have heard of some other folks' ideas of what the future could be, and I invite more. I have ideas of my own. Send or call yours in and I'll write them up in a future column. I would go on now but for lack of space.

Craftsmanship on wood and metal

Just the other week, Bill Bower of Bower's Antiques showed up at our back door bearing a gift. Well, technically it wasn't a gift, since we've paid him for it, but for the price, and considering the craftsmanship and love that went into that labor, we truly felt we had been given something of great value.

That something was the restoration of a miniature rocking chair as old as or older than I am. Originally it had been painted red and had an old-fashioned straw-woven seat. I sat in it as a boy. Since then, the paint was badly chipped and the seat unraveled. Bill saw to the task of chipping off the remaining paint and refinishing the chair to bring out its natural wood color instead of the artificial red. His wife and number one assistant, Helen, did the weaving. We couldn't be happier with their work.

Chatting a few days later with Bill Wilkins over at the B&D, I discovered that my and Anita's experience is not unique. Bower's Antiques has done some restoring for the Wilkinses, too, and talking to me of it, Bill Wilkins couldn't get over the quality of the work for such a reasonable price. What he thought he might try to do himself to his amateur best, he gladly turned over to a professional when he got such a fair estimate. Ask about it next time you're in Bill and Donna's store. We are lucky to have such talented restorers in the neighborhood.

Imagine how happy we were, then, to hear last week that Bill Bower has no more cancer. His recent heart attack, as much as it concerned all his family and friends at the time, was perhaps a blessing, since it led to the detection of this slow-growing cancer, and to its elimination before it had spread uncontrollably. I'm told that Bill himself was into the B&D, telling his news, and Anita says it's the talk of the town, so I guess I'm safe in reporting that it's true. If you hadn't heard before now, you can say you heard it here first.

Now, the folks at Bower's Antiques aren't the only good craftsmen in or around Leopold. Jerry and Tim up at Viking Truck and Auto Repair, for example, barely half a block away from us, have helped me keep my car on the road, and that's something I don't take lightly. I took some auto shop in junior high, and, as hard as I concentrated, I couldn't get a smidgen of mechanical know-how to stick in my brain. Jerry says he's admired my ability to turn a phrase on paper; well, I'm impressed by his ability to make sense of the mysteries under a car's hood. I was just thinking of the Viking crew again, anyway, as I looked up the hill and noticed their new sign, which adds a nice touch.

Jerry has told me before about his Houston connection. He used to drive trucks down that way during the oil boom years. That ended when the bottom went out from under the oil prices a few years back, so now we have him here. That's good news for the neighborhood.

Tim would seem to be Jerry's right hand, and both men are always pleasant to talk to. I appreciate their friendliness and honesty, since in a garage I might easily be lied to. They don't talk down to me and I don't talk down to them. They understand that community consists of a variety of people with different gifts to share with each other. No one is more or less valuable than another.

After my springtime accident in Tell City, Jerry referred me to Tim, who he said was his body man. That must be true, because Tim did a good job of putting my front fender back in place for a price that hurt much less than the bruising my pride took when I realized that half of the county had been witness to my misfortune. "It's not pretty," Jerry told me when he showed me the finished product, but it was fine by me. Of the five or six cars I've driven since courting and marrying Anita eleven years ago, only one has been pretty, and it was pretty no more after Marshall, Texas.

If you don't know the histories of my Tell City or Texas accidents, ask my students, who got the blow by blow on each one. After the last one, a girl in sophomore English exclaimed, "Mr. Sanders, you have such bad luck!" Sometimes I do, but not always. I have done nicely enough in my recent choice of community, neighbors and friends, both in and out of the classroom.

Long-lost relations:
Found at the church fundraiser

Last Sunday, the day of the big fundraising picnic up at
St. Augustine's, the family and I received a surprise visit from
long-lost relatives. They were on their way to see the quilts just
up the road from us. Their Christian names are Alice and Hazel,
my dad's two aunts that I remember visiting when I was little. I
don't remember seeing them much since then, unless it was at
Grandma Evelyn's funeral.

I wrote "long-lost" for the romantic effect. Really, I suspect
they have always known their own whereabouts (living now in
Tell City), and had I thought to investigate I might have found
out, too. Hazel, Alice, and Evelyn, my dad's mom, were born the
daughters of William and Henrietta Chapple, whose farm out by
Tobinsport I remember vividly. Evelyn married Everett Sanders,
and later Lindsey Reed. Alice and Hazel married (I think) two
brothers, Taylor and Jesse Stith. Jesse was killed in WWII when
my dad was just a boy. Hazel, if I am not mistaken, is now a
Polk.

Evelyn was the remarkable and strong woman who connected
us grandkids to the paternal line even when we lived far away. I
remember being many times at her country house out in
Tobinsport and eating her country food. She collected dogs and
cats, and she never threw anything away, so her house had a lot
in it to see. It was hard to say good-by to her a few years ago
when she suddenly died.

I only met Grandpa Everett, who was not with her then, a
time or two, up at the house that my dad tells me Earl and Ruth

Loesch now live in. I mentioned once that it is listed in the county surveys as the Frank Sanders farm. When I visited, my great-grandparents were still there, the cheerful and toothless John Franklin and the forever rosy-cheeked Verna Artimissa Ryan. I remember the winding staircase and the ice cream she always had for us to eat. I remember once being introduced there to Everett.

The Chapple farm was back of a long dirt road that dug through the soil and was flanked by high-rising trees with their bulky roots emerging from earthen walls. I remember riding in the family station wagon back to the house, past the little cemetery and through the imposing trees, which to my Gothic imagination was like a scene out of one of the spooky, black-and-white horror movies that I used to stay up on Friday nights to watch, or out of Bram Stoker's *Dracula*. There were no spooks in the old farm house, though, and again the country food and family togetherness were good and warm.

I remember all of this and some more. I recall Uncle Harry, who was always laughing through yellowed teeth and used to sell Tropicana orange juice, if memory serves me well. I remember Dad's sisters and their husbands, though I don't often see them. I have internalized the tale of my dad's great-grandpa Napoleon Bonaparte Sanders (no kidding!), born precisely a century before me in 1858 — somewhere in the bowels of Kentucky. He was a skinny man and his friends called him Bones, or Boney. (In Argentina when I was still thin, people used to call me Flaco, which means the same thing.) What I don't know for a fact about him leaves room for imaginative embellishment, and you already know that I like to dress up the truth a little from time to time.

So even though I haven't kept up with Dad's family as intimately as with Mom's, it's a family that has shaped me in ways that I probably don't completely know. It's a family I want to know (or imagine) more fully. So it was really nice to hear, if only briefly, from Alice and Hazel. Perhaps now we won't be strangers.

As for the Leopold picnic, there were quilts being raffled and a lot more. Since Jonathan was fresh back from his three special weeks at the School for the Blind in Indianapolis, the family and I were all together here for the weekend, and we strolled up the hill for a while and tried for some cakes and ice cream. The kids bought the ice cream but failed to win a cake. I was sorely disappointed in their performance.

I was pleased, however, to see several of my students and acquaintances from Lear Pool and its surroundings. Paul Hagman mentioned reading my column, so I figure he deserves to see his name in here. I think of him as the ever-smiling, fun-loving custodian. His daughter Stephanie was there selling shirts with Lesly Guillaume and Kristy James — all three from last year's Spanish III class. I also caught two of the guys from that class, cousins Rick and Stan Hubert. They were startled when I addressed them in Spanish, but came through in the clutch with the appropriate phrases. I told Stan I enjoyed reading his fiction-essay in the paper the other day.

I was also proud to see Kristy's name and picture in connection with her recent trip to Washington D.C. with the Indiana Rural Electric group. Since returning home, she's been selling peaches (last year, she picked them) just off 37 before the Leopold south exit. She says she enjoyed everything in Washington immensely, including a chat with Congressman Lee Hamilton, but especially the nighttime tour of various monuments. She was especially struck by the Vietnam War Memorial, which she found "astonishing." It just went on and on. Few of our families, I imagine, remain untouched by the loss of someone who has gone before us in one of our fighting campaigns.

Best wishes to my good friend from around Bandon, Brent Lechner, as the Air Force takes him off to Germany. May he know peace, and his greatest challenge be to learn the language.

Introducing my friends Braulio and Tasha

Between thunderstorms last Thursday evening, while the kids and I were immersed in the rhythms of James Whitcomb Riley, we were interrupted by the jarring ring of the telephone. Imagine my surprise upon hearing simultaneously, from different regions of the country, the voices of my old friends Braulio and Tasha.

I owe this three-way communication to one of Ma Bell's latest technological marvels, which, like the VCR and word processor before it, has left me behind the times and underfunded. What little I watch on TV is of the regular networks' offering and on their schedule, and I still process my words the old-fashioned way, on the manual Smith-Corona that my parents gave me sixteen years ago when I was in high school. I back it up with liberal doses of liquid paper and grumbling.

Braulio, anyway, who I can't resist telling you is the silver-haired ghostwriter for, among others, Stephen King (What! You didn't think Steve could turn it all out himself, did you?), is my alter ego and writing mentor. Tasha is a defected poet and circus performer from the former Soviet Union. I have always been able to count on Braulio and Tasha to set me straight. Believe me.

"Listen, Brett," Braulio said, "I'm the first in the world to admire a good yarn, but bilingual cows reciting Spanish poetry in the middle of Hoosier National Forest? I can buy the ghosts, but Brett, those cows?"

"And you're getting sloppy with facts, too," Tasha cut in. "Here you get on Ruth's case for writing 'B-r-e-*t*' for 'B-r-e-*t-t*,' and this week you put 'L-e-s-*l-y*' for 'L-e-s-*l-e-y*.' How do you think that poor Guillaume girl feels?"

"That's for sure," Braulio added. "Reminds me of the time in high school you put 'R-o-l-*f* S-a-m-u-e-l-s-*e*-n' in print as 'R-o-l-*p-h* S-a-m-u-e-l-s-*o*-n.' Do you enjoy looking foolish?"

Finally I got a word in edgewise.

"First," I said, "I was confused. It's the parents' fault for spelling their kids' names differently: *ie*, *ey*, just *y*. Second, since when do you get the *News*? And third, you didn't know me in high school — how do you know about that pipsqueak Samuelsen?"

"Shifting the blame again!" Tasha guffawed. "You sound positively Presidential."

"So I'm ashamed. Embarrassed. There."

"Besides," Braulio added. "We know all about you. Haven't you seen your national ratings? I've heard talk, myself, of a syndicate buying you up. Your fame has spread: people who want to know buy the *News*. And that ghost story's really tops — not that Steve and I couldn't improve on it a bit."

So it was the haunted hotel they wanted to talk about. At least it wasn't the law, as Anita feared, to haul me away for my thoughtless trespassing or some parent telling me she's suing because her child followed my bad example and fell through the second-story floor.

I did ask my readers to call in with their suggestions for the hotel, after all, so I had set myself up for this.

"You know, Brett," Tasha said then, "I really think that place sounds like it would make a swell artists' colony, if I could just talk Brau and Stevie into putting up the money. That's my dream for the place. Artists and poets and troubadours would come from miles around and have a safe haven. Just think of all the creativity and sharing! We could have readings, showings — sell crafts, art, chapbooks — I tell you, Brett, Leopold could become to Perry County what Nashville [Indiana] is to Brown County."

"I'll admit there's been talk down here about promoting tourism," I answered. "And just a while back, Bill Bower was saying he was sure he could fix the place up in three months, if he had half a mind to."

"Did he say that part about having half a mind to?" Braulio put in.

"Well, no, and I'm sure he has a full mind, if any."

"There you go again, Brett," Tasha said, "but I'm glad to hear someone thinks it can be done. I've heard the rumors that it's beyond repair, but you know what they say: once you're committed to the task, the probabilities change in your favor."

"I heard earlier that Bill Wilkins, if he ends up buying the place after all, was thinking of tearing it down and putting up a car wash," Braulio said. "Now there's an interesting notion, and if you have the foresight to keep this haunted hotel story going, then Steve and I can really make a killing. A variation on *Christine*, you know, only this time it's not the car that wreaks havoc but the car wash itself, possessed by the hotel's dispossessed spirits. I tell you, Brett, there are possibilities here. Forget the writers' colony baloney — I'll set you and Tasha up somewhere else if it comes to that."

"Well, I don't know, Brau," I said. "I think the haunted car wash wouldn't go down really well with the local residents. And as much as I like the other idea, I don't know. I think Bill Bower was thinking more along the lines of some apartments."

"That's okay," Tasha said. "At least then you're not tearing down your county's heritage. I heard about Cannelton and that courthouse thing, and the historical preservation law they passed."

"Yes," I said. "It's like Robert Hughes's book I've been reading during the Olympics, *Barcelona*. You know, in that city with all their tradition of architecture they have what Hughes calls an 'ideology of preservation'? 'Taste cannot be legislated,' Hughes writes, 'but at least the integrity of the past can be.' As in Cannelton, existing structures are protected by law. 'Before he can touch a brick, the owner of a building must prove to the Ajuntament's [City Council's] satisfaction that it is not of historical significance.' That's a clear voice for preservation."

"Preservation, presersmation," Braulio muttered. "Give me a blockbuster on the charts and film rights in the pocket."

"Don't listen to that shallow materialist," Tasha said. "The apartments sound nice, but think about it. Hotel rooms and an arts and crafts shop, with the proper backing, could still keep the right person in business."

"And if the place can't be restored after all," I added, "the car wash would be a perfect complement to Jerry's shop across the street."

Sleep on it.

Tom Wolfe and the demolition derby

When you read this, Perry Central students will be eleven days shy of the first day of school. Teachers will officially report three days earlier. For some of us, though, practitioners of what is vulgarly considered a nine-month profession, summer is already out. I would wager that many of us are involved on and off since early June in actual preparatory school activities.

My mind has been churning with ideas since before Mexico, but I'm back in the classroom in a big way since a full four weeks before the kids arrive. I mention this because the idea for this column arises from the planning last week of a lesson in sophomore literature.

The writing at lesson's center is a fast-paced essay by Tom Wolfe on the American-bred sport of the demolition derby. It occurs to me that this piece, which we didn't cover last year, may tickle the fancy of some of my dirt bike riders and speed demons, bless their souls.

Tom Wolfe is a relatively young writer and proponent of the so-called New Journalism, which is fiction-paced nonfiction writing. It's the plain facts, as the writer interprets them, put forth in a highly readable fashion. Wolfe is the author of *The Right Stuff* and, more recently, the novel *Bonfire of the Vanities*, neither of which I have actually read.

This essay grabs hold of me right away, though, and makes, I imagine, a fair introduction to his style. The rough-and-tumble saga of the demolition derby brings to mind sundry thoughts and memories of Leopold and the Big Beyond.

First, the speed demons of Leopold. Living right here by the square, we get a lot of activity, a good amount of it occurring after the midnight hour. Being old people as we are (relatively speaking), we have not always appreciated the squeal of tires and smell of rubber waking or keeping us from sleep. The tires spin on and on in place, wearing off yet more layers of rubber. As the cars take off, then, side by side around the bend by Lonnie Goffinet's house, we fear the drag race may become Leopold's own demolition derby.

My irritation reminds me of the folks in E.C. Roberts's English, Indiana, described in his entertaining book *Memories of Main Street* (check it out of the local library). First, in those simpler days when what few cars there were went twenty miles per hour, a newspaper editorial complained about being overrun by speed demons; earlier, another editorial griped about speedsters raising dust on horses: one of the two suggested locking the young offenders up. Then, when weekend revelers got loud and rowdy at Main Street after the midnight hour, would-be sleepers stuck their heads out of their windows and said to shut up. The party crowd, responding somewhat in kind, told their reprovers something more saucy than I can exactly remember.

Some things never change. Young and old, we have our ways of asserting our personal freedom or sovereignty.

That thirst for freedom and excitement must have been what motivated my friend Carl Rahkonen, whom I knew in Bloomington, to enter the demolition derby in Utah where he grew up. Now Carl's a successful, if not sedate, husband-father-professor at Indiana University of Pennsylvania. I can hear his gleeful cry and see his blond hair in the wind as he tears after another jalopy.

It's this sense of freedom, of controlling one's own destiny for that fleeting moment, that so many of my students write about in relation to their dirt bike riding. Students write well when they write about what they love. Some teachers get off on dirt bikes, too, or on hunting or fishing or whatever. Kurt Cooper says he relaxes and thinks on his bike. One student wrote of being Michael Jordan as he soared through the air before his own basketball hoop, as I used to imagine myself as Kareem Abdul-Jabbar. Now I get the same kind of thrill when I write a bold new story (some day I will make it!) and put it in the mail, defiant of the rejection slip that odds say will follow.

I think that's what the loud cars and loud music are really about, though the blatant publicness of the noise doesn't generally move me to such gentle reveries. Part of my freedom, the freedom to think, is infringed upon by the blaring music or engines. Still, in certain moods, I like loud music, too. One of my pleasantest memories of Mexico is a conversation over dinner with Travis Esarey and Lesly Wilkins, on the transcendent merits of folk to heavy metal music. I have to remember that I once listened to Alice Cooper. Still, people say I turned out okay.

More than that renegade rocker, anyway, I liked music like the jazz-influenced rock of the band Chicago. I just pulled out their fifth album as I was writing this and drank in those old trumpets and drums and untamed harmonies. It's not pure jazz, but the jazz is there, and it speaks to me still. "Jazz stands for freedom," says pianist Dave Brubeck. "It's supposed to be the voice of freedom: Get out there and improvise, and take chances, and don't be a perfectionist — leave that to the classical musicians."

The dark side of this freedom urge, of course, is when we let it be turned in against ourselves, as in the Los Angeles riots.[2] There is the violent nature of the demolition derby, reflected too in the blood-lust of spectators at such events as the Indianapolis 500 or the sprint car races at Salem, Indiana.

The year my Grand Prix racing hero Jochim Rindt died in a crash in Europe, and Indianapolis drivers faced serious accidents at home, I also witnessed at close range a deadly crash at Salem, Indiana. That was 1973. The car-wrapped-around-tree held interest, but I had never expected to watch a man's death. My enthusiasm for the sport quickly faded in the face of that savage reality.

One hopes that the sometimes misdirected enthusiasms of area speedsters might fade, too, before a single young person dies along one of our county roads, wrapped with machine around a tree's wounded form.

As a teacher, I aspire to direct young people's freedom quests in what may become more fruitful directions. At the same time, however, I would inspire them to avoid the unnecessary chains of their elders: learn the facts and discipline, but get out there and improvise, take chances.

Fly like an eagle, in the immortal words of gentle rocker Steve Miller.

2   I realize, in retrospect, that the "freedom urge" is an inadequate explanation for the rage that exploded in Los Angeles in 1992, after the Rodney King verdict; without failing to acknowledge the waste involved in the destruction of one's own community, James Baldwin suggests a better explanation in his 1955 essay "Notes of a Native Son" with its focus on the 1943 Harlem riots.

Albertine Gleeson: Pioneer woman principal

A couple of Saturday evenings past, after the family and friends and I had been into the Schweitzer Fest and dropped off last Thursday's column to the office, I received a phone call from a fan.

No, it wasn't Braulio or Tasha, but someone a lot of you probably know. So all of you doubting Thomases out there who disbelieve in talking cows, tooth fairies, and the objective truth of all of my words can verify these facts.

The caller was Avis Irvin of Cannelton, whose daughter and son-in-law, Mary Avis and Chris Seitz, live in Branchville and have been so welcoming to us since our arrival last fall back in my native county.

I have always counted on Chris for smart conversation at the lunch table, as Anita has counted on him for gardening advice delivered with an indulgent laugh, an elfish grin, and the kindness of not reminding her that she and I, to borrow a neighbor's ungentle phrase, are a couple of city idiots.

As for Mary Avis, one of my dad's former schoolmates at Cannelton High, it has been her voice on the phone so many times, inviting us to their home to join their circle of friends at New Year's Eve or to go out square dancing. She is an excellent hostess, and always a jolly person to chat with.

It almost seemed as if it were Mary Avis on the phone again the other day. You certainly hear her in her mother. I didn't recognize that at first — perhaps because the voice was asking me if this was the Sanders residence and if she could speak to Brett Sanders — but after she identified herself it became obvious.

To hear her laugh as we talked, then, was to hear her daughter's familiar laughter. It was like New Year's Eve again, seeing and hearing Nancy Spencer and Elaine Seibert at the same time, vaguely thinking that they sure look and talk alike — then learning almost by accident that they are sisters. Yes, now it all makes sense. I have to remember this is Perry County, where we are all mostly related to each other.

So it was good to hear from Mary Avis's mother, and to read Norma June Frakes's informative report before that of Mary Avis and Chris's Hawaii adventures.

Avis Irvin — the last name reminds me of another intertwining of county relationships, that Mary Avis Seitz and Darryl Irvin are cousins — called to say she enjoys my column and to ask if anyone had ever told me about some other historical Leopold residents whom she hadn't seen me mention.

No, they hadn't, I said — at least none that I got a clear handle on at the time — so she left me with one significant story. I'm always happy to hear any other.

She told me, then, about Albertine Gleeson, who was principal of the old high school — Oil Township High — before the nice building Chris and I now teach in was complete.

Albertine lived out here in Leopold, together with a sister and a brother. None of the three ever married, I am told. Albertine would be somewhere around 100 years old if she were still alive today. Back when Albertine started out, Avis reminded me, there wasn't so much formal training required before she could do what she did, but she still took classes in the summer to better herself professionally.

"She was influential in the school," Avis said, "because she was such a good teacher, as well." It was unusual too, she added, that as a woman she found herself in the traditionally male domain of principal.

Presumably, we have made certain progresses in education over the years. This isn't the place to determine what they are or aren't.

In any case, Albertine's story reminds us that those who preceded us have left, in many instances, a legacy of greatness that should inspire us. They may not have had the same length of training — Laura Ingalls was not sixteen when she first taught, and my great-grandpa Frank Sanders had completed eighth grade, if I remember well — but they passed demanding exams and then harnessed their creativity to lead children toward knowledge.

We teach in a different world, with a different set of challenges, but the basic challenge — to harness our creativity to lead children toward knowledge — remains.

Speaking of Frank Sanders, schoolteacher-farmer, Avis told me she knew him and Verna quite well. "Verna was about as pretty a lady as there ever was," she said, to which sentiment I readily agreed.

At past 80 years old, with her rosy cheeks and smile, she is remembered as the spring flower of Tobin Township, and now I know it was not just family that thought so. Avis remembers her as being immaculate in the way she would present herself — she always wore gloves and hat when no one else did.

Thanks to Avis and so many others who have put in their good words about my column. Yes, as long as you're asking for it, I'll keep it up and, contrary to Anita's wifely concern, I haven't noticed that my head has outgrown the sporty new Mexican hat you may have seen me wearing.

1992: Talk of the County (Columnist)

Deaths in the family

News of Anita's mom's sudden death the other week came on the heels of our painful, week-and-a-half parting from our first family cat. It was like kicking us when we were already down.

The loss of mother and mother-in-law is a graver matter than the loss of a cat, but to insist on the point is to diminish the very real love that is nevertheless involved in that latter relationship. Those of you who have ever loved and lost a pet understand my feelings.

Anita's mom, Mary Rent, died of massive heart failure at about 1 a.m. on August 13, peacefully asleep. While originally from the "Region," up toward Hammond in Lake County, she had lived the past ten years in Cass, a small town on the fringes of Dugger in Sullivan County.

She had loved that southern region and wanted to be laid to rest there. She enjoyed the country atmosphere and liked going fishing to relieve stress. She was the only woman in a male-dominated community to take on the mighty Amax Coal Co. and force compliance with lawful consideration of the local population. She had come to admire and be admired by several neighbors and would often comment on the extreme warmth and hospitality of southern as opposed to northern Hoosiers.

Her biggest fault, perhaps owing somewhat to her rough, urban breeding, was a distrust of outsiders that made her protectiveness of family seem almost fanatical. That was the labyrinth I stumbled into as I proposed to steal away her second-to-oldest daughter.

Lately, she seemed more accepting and we were more at peace, though I see a lot of her distrustful legacy reflected in the mourning of several of her family.

The cat was put to sleep on the 11th. We were so touched a few days later to receive the note from Dr. Alan Decker and staff at the Greenwood Animal Hospital in Tell City. "What was once enjoyed we can never lose," it read. "All that we love deeply becomes a part of us."

Patches had a little-understood malady called feline infectious periodonitus, or something like that. He had suddenly become sick.

When he didn't respond to the antibiotics after a couple of trips to the vet, we left him there for more observation. He never came home.

The blood test revealed damaged kidneys and liver. F.I.P. was the apparent diagnosis. Nothing else made sense. There was no cure.

Just like that our lively, two-year-old spitfire had wasted away to a mere shadow of his former self. One day he had diarrhea and was given medicine for worms.

Two days later, he was listless and weak. We found him lying in his litter box. We would set him back on a rocking chair and give him water, which he lapped gingerly out of a shallow saucer. He wouldn't touch solid food.

The contrast to his former self was startling. When we moved into the Coopers' house last September, Patches was a homeless gray and white shorthair living in the barn out back. We eased him into the basement and finally up the stairs.

He came to trust us and was soon one of the family. He would chase circles around the house and pounce on us like a playful shark. His jaws were sharp.

If I moved my hand quickly enough, I could give him the play he needed and keep from getting hurt, but occasionally he would get me. Then, scratched or slightly bleeding, I would get a hand towel to keep up the game, dangling it in place of my fingers.

Sometimes Patches would just sit and be petted, purring contentedly and licking me with his sandpaper tongue. When he licked me, it was as if I were just an extension of his own body, which he was cleaning. Usually, though, he was a livewire, a young cat and by no means sedate.

He knew when we were eating and was always there to ask for his portion with pitiful, big, green eyes, peering over table's edge or one of our laps. Anita would run him off or throw him a piece of chicken. The scraps came often enough to keep him coming back.

By the time we were losing him, he no longer did any of that. His expressive eyes became transparently sad and pleading. From his looks, I think he thanked us for our care, and I'm glad he didn't die homeless and alone, but his uncharacteristic passiveness tore at my heart.

On his last morning, we all stood around him where he lay huddled and forlorn, in obvious pain, on the doctor's table, and wept. Can you imagine that some heartless soul had suggested we save a few dollars and dump him along a county road in a ditch?

We might as well do the same to a sick child. I was in full mourning for Patches up through the moment of my mother-in-law's dying. I'm not sure I'm out of it still.

The simple truth is that the love of an animal will bring out the best and most tender in the majority of us.

When I was growing up, my dad and I didn't usually have a deep understanding between us. Once I braked to miss a squirrel and totaled his car; he hardly spoke to me for several months.

But when we lost our dogs, he would cry. Once, moved to action by a loving spirit, he laid his hands on a trembling old dog's head and asked God to relieve its suffering. In that second, the dog, who had spent the last thirteen years with us, gave up the ghost.

That is the clearest miracle I've ever witnessed, wrought by the faith of a man who life had taught to affect toughness but was now inspired by the sweetness of devotion. I've never loved my dad more than in that moment.

The presence of an animal is a real comfort in our sorrow or affliction. Up at Sullivan County while we waited for the extended family, so the children and husband could decide on Mary's final arrangements, I took up with the kitten that Anita's and my little niece had picked up at a yard sale.

Grandma had been its primary caretaker, I gather, and right then I needed its care for myself.

"Don't touch that cat," one of Anita's brothers said to me, "it's mean." But I ignored the warning and kept on courting its attention. Its meanness, as I suspected, was just playfulness — to me, it was a younger incarnation of Patches.

It wanted someone to chew on, all in play, so I obliged, moving my fingers back and forth at lightning speed to avoid too sharp a bite. When its teeth did sink in, they were younger and milder than Patches's teeth and never really hurt me.

Then it just settled into my lap and went to sleep while I petted it. Anita's brothers marveled at how I'd tamed it. "Do you have a way with animals?" one of them asked, then picked it up himself and petted.

Pretty soon I noticed that just about everyone in the room, in need of reassurance and calm in those painful moments of loss, had taken the kitten in their arms.

The rest of the family arrived, finally, and the oldest brother's wife fixed herself a sandwich first and then went straight for the kitten. What else should she have done?

It was the only action that would really have made any sense at that moment, much more sense than the protracted human agony that was yet to follow through the earthly parting with Mary.

Autumn reflections and inspiration

When Mary Jeanne first spoke to me about moving my column out of rural news, she asked me if I had an idea of what to call it. I didn't.

I toyed with a couple of unsatisfactory ideas, mostly tongue-in-cheek — "The World According to Brett," for instance — and finally thought I'd turn to my readers for better suggestions.

That was before the students came back to school, though. I am always inspired, in fresh and unexpected ways, by the interaction with students, whether directly by their instruction of me or indirectly by my various attempts at instructing them.

These ideas often come to us suddenly, as Mary Jeanne was commenting to me. When we're not even thinking about it, in a moment of epiphany, as it were, the perfect title or phrase or sentence comes to us — revelation that until then, for all of our deliberation, has eluded us.

This one came to me as twenty-four English students and I were chatting under the trees in front of Perry Central on Wednesday, August 26.

Gazing out expansively over the surrounding landscape — cow pastures, cornfields, and woodland carved out of the natural territory of Hoosier National Forest — we meditated about our fair county's being, for us, the center of a universe and an experience.

All writers write from the vantage point that their imagination is centered in at the time of writing. Annie Dillard, first of the essayists I was introducing under those trees, wrote this time from the center point of an Ecuadorian village; E. B. White, the second of them, from a New England town where he was keeping a public journal and farming the land.

E. B. White, who our children know fondly as the author of such wise and simple classics as *Charlotte's Web* and *Stuart Little*, wrote for a magazine column called "Talk of the Town."

As I was telling this to my students, who were writing it dutifully into their notebooks, I experienced the silent revelation I was just suggesting to you. I should call my column "Talk of the County."

The purest sort of homage to Mr. White is intended, and my new, expanded beat allows me to sharpen my essays on whatever theme while remaining faithful to a rural center.

Presently, after a week of classes and of new beginnings, I have been sitting with *One Man's Meat*, White's book of essays from which the short selection in our literature book is taken. This is a necessary measure to keep one's battery charged up: read something unassigned, something one loves, even if it means sitting up till three in the morning to do it.

I checked this book out of the high school library and observed that I am the first person to do so since 1976. This is a book that merits revisiting in the 1990's.

My students have chosen well for their first book reviews. Authors ranging from Victor Hugo to Emily Brontë to Cervantes. Topics of historical interest such as Kent State.

Perhaps some one of them will turn back to E. B. White. They are asked to read once per semester from my prepared list of authors, twice from their own mental lists. It is good to read a lot from what one already loves, but also, occasionally, to try something new, fresh, unexpected.

Tuesday and Wednesday of that first week, perhaps Thursday, were my peak teaching days. Monday was like any other first day, a necessary evil. By Friday, I was at the height of my characteristic absentmindedness and began to wonder if my students' sweetness this year was more on account of their good natures than of my brilliant instruction.

If you ever find me wandering around at night on some country road, I confided to a few of the students who already know me from last year, apparently confused and turned around, please take me by the hand and lead me home to Anita. She will be grateful.

She worries that I'm going to lose it completely like Don Quixote, the knight of La Mancha, putting down his books to go fight windmill-giants and invisible enchanters.

I've yet to put on rusty armor and mount a steed, but I did show up in partial Mexican regalia to see Perry Central defeat North Harrison in football that Friday night.

Afterward I felt rejuvenated, less unsteady, though I still always need the weekend to brace my mind against the next Friday. Thank God for an occasional breather.

At the game, I ran into my former student and ace reporter Phillip Northernor, so I know he's filled you in on the essential facts of the evening. That leaves me to wrap this up with the essential reveries, or at least the ones that come to mind at this writing.

The fall season, with its shadow of approaching cold and storm, is a time of gathering — of gathering songs, community, warmth.

The farmers in their fields gather their harvests — the last corn and pumpkins are already in from Anita's garden, and bonfires, hayrides, and hot apple cider may follow — but the high school football field is the central autumn gathering place of the songs, community, and warmth I speak of.

We are all there, those of us back in school and others whose hearts remain with us. The coaches shout, the players grunt, and fans and cheerleaders cheer. In other corners, people visit and children, elementary sweethearts, drink hot chocolate from a single cup but out of two straws.[3]

Amidst flashes of green — Perry Central Commodore green — appear the common scenes and the eccentric ones. This is the setting in which I first met Phillip's brother, Brent Lechner, with his longish hair, colorful bandana, and Woodstock-era demeanor.

It's where, more recently, people saw a man sporting a cactus-woven hat and Maya green *serape*, a sort of wrap-around blanket or poncho brought back from Mexico.

It's all of our diversity, woven together with such events as these as backdrop, that finally enwraps us in the cohesive warmth we call community.

The performance of the marching band, small and modest as it may be, is an especially sweet moment. Several of the girls and a couple of boys, I recognize from class.

The sound of the horns comes, tentative but pure. The glow and occasional laughter on the young faces gives off a warmth of their own.

In some future day, when belonging to a band is as encouraged and socially rewarding as being on the football team is presently, we may have greater numbers of our boys and girls participating. Bands win prizes, too, though that's not the reason for having them.

As for football, whether one knows a lot, a little, or nothing at all about how it's played, it feels good to be part of the scene surrounding a high school game.

There's something inherently wholesome about the event. The game itself may at times seem unnecessarily violent, and the non-competitor's thirst for the vicarious gratification he gets from his team's winning record is hard on boys and coaches and even academics.

But all of that is another matter. The bottom line is that

community needs some event to bring it together. In Perry County, in the fall of the year, it just happens that the biggest of those is the social event we call high school football.

3   The elementary sweethearts observed here were Jonathan, my son, and fellow teacher Darryl Irvin's eldest daughter, Julie. Their brief romance did not survive the autumn season. Several years later, while she was still in high school, her family and community were heartbroken to lose her to an automobile accident.

Dancing on Ruth Ann's grave:
Life, death, and the will to meaning

"Life," according to an unknown humorist-philosopher, "is something that happens while you're looking the other way."

Thus quotes Brent Lechner, in any case, at the end of his first letter to me from Germany. A wonderful letter, incidentally, in which he lyrically sings of the gentle rain and wooded beauty around the base where he is stationed. At the last, after his signature, he adds without comment that peculiar quotation.

At some moments more than at others — and this is one of those moments — such words invade one's heart with a certain poignancy. Fresh from personal losses already mentioned in an earlier column, Anita and I confront the bittersweet experience of our extended Perry Central family.

Life, within a rapid three-day period before the dawning of a second week of classes, was thrice threatened in a big way. Miraculously, the two girls lived to tell their families the tale. One man and his family were not so lucky.

Many of you who read this will already know the stories. Of the roadside accident that wreaked havoc on the bodies of Rachel Gehlhausen and Sara Heerdink, and demolished the truck they were thrown from. Of the freakish death by lightning of Ted Lamon, Jr., who was out scouting deer near his home in Doolittle Mills.

This is not a reporting, then, but an attempt toward interpreting, a questioning of life's — and death's — meaning. No one of us is the proverbial sage atop a mountain, equipped with ready answers, but we all have asked and will continue asking the difficult questions. Each day is a new interpreting of what's behind and before us.

Psychologist Viktor E. Frankl, who as a boy survived the suffering of the Nazi death camps, observes in his wise and readable book, *Man's Search for Meaning*, that suffering, whether great or small, "completely fills the human soul and conscious mind."

Still, through a "will to meaning," the greatest and smallest of our sufferings can be overcome. Also, he contends, if the smallest matter brings such an intense suffering, isn't it logical as well "that a very trifling thing can bring us the greatest of joys?"

I know that coin, as most of us do, from both sides. Both the sorrow and the joy of it.

As a desert poet-philosopher once said, there has to be an opposition in all things: you can't appreciate the good without recognizing the bad, nor health without experiencing sickness, nor joy without knowing your share of sorrow.[4]

This is the undeniable condition of all of us. What we make of it may determine our ultimate happiness.

The joy of this condition, I experienced two Fridays past while visiting with Russell and Rita Gehlhausen and their daughter at the Owensboro-Daviess County Hospital. The trifling little thing that filled my soul was Rachel's beautiful smile, so missed by members of her Spanish class on the morning of the accident. The smile told me that she would be okay, which was all that mattered.

Later, as I carried my own sleeping daughters from the TV to their beds, I was conscious of the fragility of their existence, too, rejoicing in the privilege of sharing it with them if only for a fleeting moment.

I have not made Sara's acquaintance, but I know we all felt the same joy when she returned recently to attend a volleyball game and a day of school.

Her full mending will take time, and Rachel's a bit more time, but we rejoice that there is a mending to take place. These miracles are not trifling to anyone who loves another being.

The sorrows are not trifling, either, and they touch us all, if not each of us every time to the same extent. I didn't know Ted Lamon, but I have worked in the same building with his wife, Sheila, and read her reports in the paper.

As I drove away from the funeral home in English that Tuesday evening, the sorrow seemed to fill my soul, too, even though I hadn't known him.

How can any of us convey to Sheila and her family the depths of our caring? As I drove away, I was filled with a sense of the apparent futility of any effort to give needed comfort.

Also, I thought of Brent's cryptic postscript to me, and imagined that life really is like that. Something, as it were, that just happens to us, to all of us, as we're caught short dreaming.

In moments of inexplicable sorrow, we may well come to question all we've held true about divine justice and a hereafter, about the meaning or rightness of things. This is not a preaching, but an observation of how we are. I wondered about these things anew — about the uncertainty of what I believe or know — during the car ride home from English.

So all of us, at one time or another, may be asking the same question that Robert Fulghum, in his book *It Was on Fire When I Lay Down on It*, poses to a living Greek philosopher: "What is the meaning of life?"

The philosopher, first gazing into the questioner's eyes and gauging his sincerity, answers by reference to the example of the fragments of a shattered mirror he had played with as a child, discovering with no little fascination that he could reflect light with it into "dark places where the sun would never shine."

Later, as a man, he understood that he was like that mirror. Not himself the source of light, truth, or understanding, but able to reflect it "into the black places of the hearts of men — and change some things in some people."

"Perhaps others may see and do likewise," he says. "This is what I am about. This is the meaning of my life."

A touching example of this, to me, is an episode of the TV program *Northern Exposure*, in which the young Native American filmmaker, Ed, as an expression of love toward the older shopkeeper, Ruth Ann, presents her with a plot of land with a view, where she might some day lay down her bones and give eternal peace to her spirit.

Then, in response to his sweet gesture, she performs the sweetest act imaginable. She starts right there to dance.

"What are you doing?" her innocent-faced companion asks.

"Why, I'm dancing on my grave," she answers matter-of-factly, "I may never have a chance like this again."

So he begins dancing with her, dancing and laughing with her on her own grave. The camera moves away from them into the distance.

With those simple gestures, like mirrors reflecting light into each other's souls, they have each performed for the other an act of almost unimaginable kindness.

Ruth Ann, by diffusing the moment's natural sadness, has helped Ed come to terms with the inevitability of her eventual dying, a thought that has lately been troubling him.

He, at the same time, has shown her how deeply, to at least one fellow mortal, her living has really mattered.

Thanks to Phillip Northernor, Brent's foster brother and my student, for the loan of the book with the Greek pearl of wisdom in it. The sharing of both Phillip's and Brent's lives and thoughts has mattered a great deal to me.

As for the rest, it may be that these little gestures are the best we can really do for each other. Rachel's smile is just one example, like a gentle rain falling on a wooded German landscape in late summer.

---

4   I am paraphrasing the Book of Mormon patriarch, Lehi (2 Nephi 2: 11-13).

Giving back to the rivers that run through us

While area band boosters were off supporting their high school bands at another competition, and Perry County on the whole was engaged in countless other worthy pursuits, a few of us were recently down at Sunset Park in Tell City, taking our river back home.

It was Beth Reasoner who wrote the song, "Take Me Back Home Where I Belong." A sing-along. She began singing that one and other songs sometime after one, when folks were just straggling in, and she was joined occasionally by friends.

After three, a couple of dulcimer artists from Evansville performed some bluegrass, and Beth introduced her new song again at six, just before the unveiling of the new flood wall mural. Our numbers by then were a little bigger.

The other two-thirds of the Riversong Trio were necessarily absent. Barry was off with the bands. "Hoosier Bob," resting up in a luxurious hospital room, was perhaps dreaming his own river-songs, concocting more magic for a future Franklin School Coffee House.

We all have to be somewhere. If we can't be where we want to be, we can return there, nevertheless, in imagination and spirit. I often return that way, for instance, to my Argentina, its pampas and rivers and towns; in time, through my stories, I may yet take you there.

At present, though, it's enough to be back home where I, too, belong, in Indiana, on the shores of the river that I knew first of all.

Those of us who were there that day on our Ohio, listening to Beth and the others, touring the tugboat and tooting its horn, strolling and visiting and remembering and hoping — those of us who were there could not have asked for a better day.

We were strolling through the park and through our memories, visiting with each other and with our pasts. What were we remembering? The times the Ohio River has given us and the feeling we carry of it in our hearts. What were we hoping? That our new giving to the river will be worthy of its many gifts to us.

Its gifts to us that day were a pleasant breeze and a peaceful backdrop in friendly complement to our festive spirits. The sky was blue and clear, the sun gentle but warm. The soft, greenish water seemed calm and pure.

The play of light off its surface toward sunset, when my aunt Gayle Strassell and others were being recognized for their parts in our new gift back to it, was spectacular and soothing.

"The sea was serene," I sing with my Spanish students, "serene was the sea." In this case, the river.

It was on the river that I first went fishing. Since then I can't say as I've kept to my early promise as a fisherman, but my grandpa Marion was the one who gave me at least one fish tale to tell.

He had set the line and then took me out on his boat to haul it in. I was maybe six years old. I helped him pull that whopper in, and at his house he gave me all the credit. I still have the black-and-white Polaroid snapshot, me in a crewcut holding up a fish half my size, drinking in the glory my grandpa gave me.

My memories of Grandpa not associated with the chair factory, or the house on 10th Street where he would bounce me on his knee and tell me how he'd been "b'ar huntin' with Dan'l Boone," are associated with the river. He loved the river and lived there whenever he could.

It was out in the middle of it, on a sand bar where he'd taken me and Todd and our cousins, that I got another fish tale to tell.

I guess it was Greg and I, with our younger siblings in tow, who came across it, a giant catfish stranded in a puddle of water. I don't remember if we had it for dinner or not, but I suppose we might have.

I have known other rivers, too, and loved them. The mighty Paraná in Argentina, which, with the mighty Uruguay, flows into the magnificent Río de la Plata. Other rivers, too, great and small, that I have known from books or film or song.

The gentle mountain stream that a Spanish-American poet (whose verse makes the song "*Guantanamera*") prefers to the mighty sea. The Mississippi that makes Huckleberry Finn and the musical *Big River*.

I have stood overlooking the Mississippi and felt its particular magic. I've crossed it many times. At Memphis, and somewhere north of there, south of St. Louis; again at Baton Rouge in Louisiana.

Nothing could be more stunning than the sight of it from atop a hill in Vicksburg, Mississippi, the site of a memorial to Confederate dead.

I fell in love once with Vicksburg, when I went there to interview for a teaching job I wasn't going to get. I had thought it unlikely that I could live in a state like Mississippi, with its image of race prejudice and intolerance, but changed my mind when I saw Vicksburg.

The black cab driver who retrieved me from the bus depot hoped I'd get the job, so he could take me fishing across the river in Louisiana. I felt destiny pulling. I knew I hadn't gone there for nothing.

When I didn't get the job, my heart was broken. It took a long time to get over it. I don't think I ever did until we crossed the Mississippi again to come home once more to Indiana.

We were just returning for a vacation, after the trial of a year in Houston. I drove twelve hours, pushing perhaps more than I should have, to get to Vicksburg. I was dreaming of the place again and wondering what might have been.

I had been there before by myself, and now I had to share it with some people who loved me so that they'd understand why I had loved it myself, and to make up for having not kept my promise to move them there, out of the tense uncertainty of our present life.

Vicksburg revisited was less than the memory I had carried with me. The river view was no less magnificent, but it was marred by a cussing drunkard who looked as if he might be dangerous.

The lush southern foliage was no less enchanting, but somehow the city was more ordinary. Maybe I was just too tired. Maybe, remembering earlier disillusionment, I just couldn't believe anymore in happy endings, that a black cab driver and a white teacher would really have crossed social barriers and gone off fishing.

Back from vacation in Houston, though, the phone rang, and I began to dream again. This August, back home for the past year on the river that really controls my destiny, my family and I visited with Huck Finn and the slave Jim who, in Mark Twain's book and Lincoln City's musical production, rafted together down that big muddy Mississippi and did cross those barriers.

It's good to be back on this, my own river, the one that first taught me and is again teaching me to sing. It's good to dream again.

While my dream is planted here in Perry County, though, I retain a purer perspective about places like Houston. I hope the people whose destinies are there will keep dreaming, too, so that all of us together might take home to ourselves the healing waters we need to nourish us.

Sometimes, of course, when we feel nourished enough, it's the taste of adventure we seek. Ask Kenny and Donna James, or any of their friends who were with them recently down in Tennessee, about the thrills of white water rafting.

Gary Dauby, reminding me at the flood wall mural dedication of his Leopold roots, tells of another kind of adventurer in his family tree. A distant Dauby, married and settled in Leopold, wandered off on a flatboat and never came back.

Folks thought he'd perished, but later investigations turned up some major Dauby industry somewhere in Mississippi. Guess he settled down with some other woman. Not a diversion I would necessarily recommend to anyone.

Oh, by the way, Terry Wagner drove through Lear Pool the other day. Waved to me and shouted. Said to be sure to acknowledge the fact in my column. He reminded me again at Kenny and Donna's Labor Day weekend pig roast, where Donna was showing me pictures of their trip.

Halloween pranksters and their unseasonal snowfall

County "tic-tackers," as those seasonal tricksters with their toilet paper and other mischief are known in these parts, are out in force this year, and it's not even Halloween. Come to think of it, as you're reading this it's just now October, and that paper-thin hygienic snow has already been falling in my yard and on my trees for two weeks.

At first it was merely a roll or two of toilet paper strewn through my unlocked car and across the clothesline. I hardly noticed. A few nights later, though, someone knocked on the front door to announce a job more artistically crafted.

I had just come home tired from an evening meeting. My volunteer exterior decorators were on or around the porch swing in the front yard, waiting for my return, but I didn't see them.

I went inside and they went to work. I went to bed, having neglected to give chase when they noisily announced their handiwork.

In the shower next morning, I composed a rhyme. I got dressed, then, and valiantly shoved my way through reams of hygienic paper and ruined film tape to my awaiting car. At school, I transferred my poetry from head to chalkboard:

I dreamt I'd been tic-tacked,
But that just cannot be.
Black tape and toilet paper
'Twere meant for Halloween.

My predecessor in Room I-North, Greg Moran, might well have been dreaming when, his first October in this southern wilderness, he looked out his window and thought he'd been hit by Satanists.

When I arrived here last fall to take his place, I was forewarned about this quaint little tradition, so when the pranksters did strike I was not confused about their social affiliations.

In fact, I consider that I owe the genesis of my humble career as a chalkboard rhymester to their first visit:

You've warmed our heartstrings so,
We only want to know—
Is it Charmin?

Fact is, I don't like Charmin, which is too flimsy to be functional, so I was relieved to learn it was generic. I won't tell you how much money we saved last year.

So began, in any case, my students' initiation of me into Perry County folkways, traditions from which I'd been too long divorced through years of wandering exile.

Now, I know that people in other places throw toilet paper in trees, too, but I'm not aware of the custom's having achieved anywhere else such a sanctified cult status and following as it has here.

Fascinated and slightly charmed by my students' attentiveness to me, anyway, I was amazed to learn that, in Perry County, whole families engage in this pastime.

It has gradually dawned on me that even a few school teachers and certain cafeteria personnel have been known to be in on the act.

You have to understand that this remains, for a newcomer such as I, a matter of some wonder, even of a certain clinical curiosity. I am not inclined to go on record as endorsing all of the adolescent shenanigans that I describe here (certainly not the more destructive ones I pass over).

Imagine my horror, for instance, upon learning that my mother — my very own mother, for heaven's sake! — had once taken part, herself, in such revelries.

As for me, I admit to having had my own fun, most of it last year when, to Anita's befuddled amusement, I spent the better part of October chasing swift-footed tic-tackers through the streets of Leopold.

Once, I caught up with Pat Haney, Jr. and Deana Mogan hiding on the Haneys' porch. When the rest of the gang circled around, Pat had me hide and then surprise them. I rode home on the back of the truck and they took the paper down.

Another time, when I'd been hiding out in the shed, I raised a considerable noise from Gwen Bender and Stephanie Hagman to whom I gave Kool-Aid to make up for scaring them. I didn't know that they were distracting me while the rest of the gang finished the job.

Usually, I didn't catch anyone, but huffed and puffed in the general direction of their flight. Once, I fell in a ditch, and the piece of information found an eager place in the school paper.

What I liked the most, I think, was the feeling of being welcomed and even loved. Some of the same kids who were putting toilet paper in my trees, after all, had also bought and signed a copy of the previous year's yearbook to thank me for being their teacher. This was all a heady experience after the urban warfare of teaching in Houston.

Perhaps chasing my students last year, and my continued poetry, have been sufficient thanks to them, because I'm getting too old to keep up the chase, especially in September. I have also come to wonder why no one comes back next day to clean up the mess, as I'm told is part of the chivalry of the sport.

This sport's origins, I'm also told, are connected with Halloween trick-or-treating, and so should be limited to the last day or two of October. People who don't give you a treat receive a deserved trick. I guess this was just too much fun to restrict to so small a time frame, and the democratic spirit in us led to its extension to a broader audience.

In its purest form this tradition is, more than sport, a sort of populist expression of art. The drooping toilet paper is like pure white snow, a scene foreshadowing the real winter landscape for which Bing Crosby croons. Thus it has been described to me by more than one student. The arts are indeed not dead in Perry County.

It's in this spirit of artistry, then, that I mention my recent work at our football homecoming rally, in front of the whole Perry Central student body and faculty, on Jason Sprinkle's face.

It was pie-in-the-face day, and I wanted to be sure, on behalf of all who've known him, that Jason got his fair share of it. I slapped the whipped cream on like so much shaving cream. The snowfall this time fell from us to him.

I kind of imagine that even Jason should appreciate that splendid symmetry.

Two books on humanity's ecological responsibility

Driving out into the county recently, I saw two deer at close range. A few minutes later, I saw four more at closer range, wandering together between stretches of forest land. The sight of them inspired considerable awe in me.

I am remembering that I once wanted to become a forest ranger. Then I could have lived in closer harmony with the deer, observing them not just from behind the wheel of my car.

I suppose that was an unrealistic dream, though, sort of like when, earlier, I had aspired to drive an Indy 500 race car. I can neither fix a car nor set a decent camp.

I may well become a good camper, though, before I make the race car circuit. I have entirely lost interest in the latter, though not the former.

I remember the times I camped with my dad, and wish I had inherited more of his self-assurance about outdoor activities. I always enjoyed being outdoors, but never was sure that I exactly knew what I was doing there.

If I was completely at home neither with machine nor with nature, then, with what was I at home? I guess it should be no surprise that I say with books. It is through books that I have imbibed much of the passion and longing that I feel toward a natural world I have not been totally at home in.

I recently finished a couple of books that bear special mention, both for their effect on me and their pertinence to Perry County.

I just read John Steinbeck's *To a God Unknown*. I do not have space to write an exhaustive review, but especially striking is the very Biblical concept of humanity as steward over God's creation.

"It's mine," the book's mystical hero says as he comes onto his California homestead, "and I must take care of it."

Later, when famine and drought come to the land, he thinks, "I was appointed to care for the land, and I have failed." In the book's resolution, he waits and labors lovingly until the solution finally comes to him, and rain follows.

What Steinbeck approaches through the symbolism of early humanity's reliance on mystery and ritual, Senator Al Gore approaches in his new book, *Earth in the Balance*, through an intelligent and penetrating look at the history, philosophy, and science of where we are now in relation to the natural world.

I was drawn to this book by a review last spring in *The Christian Science Monitor*. Unlike other books by politicians, the reviewer wrote, it was neither self-serving nor partisan, and besides that was the best environmental treatise to have been written since Rachel Carson's *Silent Spring*. Given that review and Mr. Gore's bid for the vice presidency, I had to read it myself.

I was not disappointed. Again, I do not have space to do much more than urge my readers to read it, too. Read it as soon as possible, regardless of what happens in November.

Central to Gore's argument, anyway, is that contemporary humanity has become estranged from the natural world, having fallen prey to a philosophy rooted in Platonic theory, that we exist separately from and above nature.

In a nutshell, this has caused us to think that we could control nature without taking any of our lessons directly from it. This has led to our present predicament, which Gore describes at length, and for which he proposes specific solutions on a global scale.

It is interesting to me that both Steinbeck and Gore have had recourse to a concept of care-giving dominion, after the Biblical model, rather than the thoughtless domination that has characterized our modern thinking.

Whichever administration is elected in November, it makes sense to me to judge it, at least in part, by how it responds, in practice, to the Democratic vice-presidential candidate's environmental proposals.

We should judge ourselves, perhaps, in a similar fashion. How strange, too, if it were from the mystical and intellectual arguments of books, rather than the simple experience of living on Earth, that we got the real driving passion to take home not only our river, but also our planet!

Greywolf family and the centrality of story

Cloudwalker and Spiritwoman Greywolf were at the Tell City Public Library the other night, sharing with area children and adults a fascinating glimpse into their Native American heritage.

Together they answered questions and showed us traditional clothes and objects that they have made themselves, and Cloudwalker told some stories.

The Greywolfs are new residents in the county, having moved here this past summer with a son and two daughters. The youngest daughter, Moonstar, is a senior at Perry Central and a member of my third-year Spanish class.

I had met Moonstar's parents once before, and felt profoundly at ease in their presence, so when Perry Central librarian Sue Knox told me of the upcoming event, I was anxious for my own children to hear the stories. I don't know whether parents or children enjoyed them more.

At the beginning, Cloudwalker, seated cross-legged on a blanket folded on the floor, explained to us that their people have always used stories rather than spanking to influence their children.

Then, while Spiritwoman stood to his side, he told some of those stories. He spoke in soothing yet animated tones, communicating with gesturing hands and skillful intonation of voice. Everyone listening was transfixed.

He told a number of stories. First, of a hungry, greedy spider who deceived a magpie, ate more than its share of raspberries, and just blew up: this story would be told to children when they did not want to share.

Another story explains why mosquitoes buzz in people's ears, and another how the strawberry came to be. A common thread throughout the tales is the Native Americans' respect for creation in all its variety.

Another theme concerns the silliness of our jeopardizing community or family for petty quarrels.

Columbus's great error, when he encountered the New World people, was in supposing they had no religion worthy of study or emulation.

I continue to wrestle with the historical enigma of Columbus, devout Catholic and determined conqueror, but I have no difficulty in acknowledging the Native people's deep spirituality, embodied for us the other night in the Greywolfs' sharing.

I like that their religion has not forgotten, as frequently our own has, that creation and creator are all bound together, every facet of them, in holy symbiosis. We must be kind to every creature, the stories say, or else lose what we have.

I liked the centrality of the story itself, and find myself wishing that we would let our own sacred stories breathe as freely, just for the narrative's sake. Can we put aside contentious dogmas long enough for the stories to work their magic on us individually?

I especially like the sacred space that each individual maintains within the Native American community, and I long for that depth of belonging in our various communities.

Cloudwalker, for instance, is a gatherer and sustainer of stories, and that alone, among his people, is justification for his being. Spiritwoman is a practitioner of the healing arts. Everyone has his or her place, and it is a valued and respected one.

In the Christian Bible, Paul speaks of the body of Christ, and of how the foot cannot say it has no need of the hand, and so forth.

Each person has a spiritual gift, necessary to the health of the whole body, yet sometimes I feel that, within our mainstream society, and within our churches, we are too busy pushing round pegs into square holes to nurture each other's natural gifts, or even know what they are.

Cloudwalker and Spiritwoman Greywolf are part of the whole of our Perry County family now, enriching us with the distinctive gifts and spirituality that they bring from their Cheyenne heritage in Oklahoma and Montana.

We are glad they are here. They promise to keep us informed, through the library, of other events they may be involved in, such as pow wows and native dances that the public can attend.

A political coming-out

In our county, if you hadn't noticed, we recently participated in a presidential election. While Indiana as a whole went Republican, we tended, in Perry County, to go Democratic, along with a lot of the rest of the country.

Consider this writing a coming out of the closet, of sorts. I, too, voted for a Democratic president. I, who was raised in a good Republican family, and whose aunt is one of the pillars of Republicanism in Tell City.

I mention this because of the spectacle of my and Anita's children in front of the TV set on November 3, cheering, along with the much-maligned liberal media, the election to the White House of a governor from Arkansas.

Their enthusiasm worried me for a couple of reasons. First, what would Mom think? More importantly, was I comfortable with their unquestioning acceptance of my tentative political judgment, which is not infallible?

Most children, after all, tend to mirror their parents' political sympathies, right or wrong.

Rather than an unbending point of view, I would prefer that we give our kids the ability to critically think. To consider all sides (expressed and unexpressed) of an issue, and grow toward making their own tentative decisions.

I would wish for our kids to understand that equally informed and caring voters may still feel differently, even altering their own course from time to time as that seems appropriate.

After all, Emerson says, in counterpoint to our day's slavish political advisors, "A foolish consistency is the hobgoblin of little minds, adored by little statesmen and philosophers and divines."

To change one's mind when to do so seems right, as Gandhi would say, is but "to grow from truth to truth."

Even so, media musings about "a new Camelot with a southern accent" being ushered in at Little Rock, through the hallelujahs and anthems of an election eve, are probably overwrought.

The history that humanity continues to live tells a different story.

The vision of Camelot, based in chivalric lore of old about King Arthur and his knights of the Round Table, does, however, provide a language of hope that suggests we can, as a people — and this is consistent, surely, with our American dream — reach more completely toward the ideal of caring for our widowed and orphaned and homeless who would share with us in that dream.

Because of my idealism, nurtured, among other ways, by my time among the poor in Argentina, I have come to admire deeply an ex-President laboring with his hands to build houses for the poor, and to feel shame at my youthful parroting of my parents' sincerest views on past Democratic figures — never mind the perceived weakness of particular administrations.

Thus, my second thoughts about the enthusiasms of my own children. Having heard aloud mere fragments of my thoughts, what if they come to think simplistically about the variety of players and issues that affect all our lives?

The retiring president is not a villain, though I choose to question some of his judgments and values.

I am troubled by the partisan besmirching of the old and sacred word *liberal*, for example, and by the cynical dismissal of substantive environmental and economic debate by lazy epithets such as Ozone Man and Mr. Tax and Spend.

Undoubtedly we could catalog more half-truths, lies, and innuendo on both sides, but I have weighed the evidence and, to the best lights available to me, declared my tentative allegiance.

As I enter now into a period of further debate and action, with the new leaders we have chosen, I will seek to hold them to the standards that, in words, they have embraced.

As for my children, let them become accountable to their own growing sense of what is right.

Holy cow! What a dream!

My old pal Braulio called the other day, and boy was he upset.

"What's this you're reporting in your talk of Perry County that I might not exist?"[5] he wanted to know. "Don't you think it's bad enough I've been hearing it from a bunch of cattle?"

Now, I have to say that the reference to cattle surprised me. You might recall back in the summer his giving me grief about my allegations of cows reciting Spanish poetry in the midst of the Hoosier National Forest.

He didn't buy it. Now he says they're talking to him. What gives?

It was Tasha who had to answer that question for me. That and any others that were to be answered just then.

"If you think I don't exist, then, what's the point of talking to you?" Braulio said petulantly, loudly blowing his nose in contradiction to that perceived denial of his being.

"You see, Brau's been having some really gnarly dreams lately," Tasha said, her interjection from a third part of the country aided, once again, by one of Ma Bell's technological marvels — three-way calling.

"Dreams?" I said, begging to be enlightened.

"Dreams of cows in a sleepy daze, looking at him through glazed eyes and droning: 'He doesn't exist, he doesn't exist, they say he doesn't exist.'"

"I see."

Braulio honked on his horn again, making his grief ever present.

"No, you *don't* see," Tasha said. "That's not the half of it." Then she took a deep breath, as if to set in for the long haul.

"You see, there are basically two dreams, and I thought maybe you could interpret them. The cows are in both, neither lean nor fatted. Just there with that depressing chorus."

"Well, I'm no Joseph of Egypt," I said, "but I'll give it my best shot."

In the interest of shortening the narrative, then, let me just summarize what Tasha told me.

The first dream involves a field of grass and a dueling of lawnmowers. The smaller of the two mowers devours the larger, and Braulio pays homage to the economy of the small one's labors.

At this point in the dream, the cows always start reciting, accompanied by the straight-set jaws of the mourners of a deposed mower, offended automatons.

The second dream involves a field of carpet and a dueling of vacuum cleaners. The smaller one does its modest work, over which the larger one proudly follows, belching up tons of dirt that the other had missed.

The smaller one, however, is not devoured, poised instead to swallow the haughty words of disappointment that pursue it.

At this point in the dream, the cows recite again, accompanied by the straight-set jaws of spurned Electrolux salespeople.

"They're disappointed, they're disappointed in him," the cattle recite in counterpoint to the other refrain about his non-existence.

"So interpret, already," Tasha demanded, while Braulio kept on blowing his nose on the other line.

"Well, those dreams are clearly meant for me," I said, "but I don't know what they mean. They seem vaguely familiar, though, as if I'd just recently been living through them, or something."

If anyone out there can interpret them for me, then, I'm all ears.

Meanwhile, let me just affirm that I do exist, and that I guess I'm forever bound to disappoint some people, myself included.

Here I am, anyway, as surely as the cows I hear calling me again. Together, I think we'll just dance a jig. While reciting the Spanish poetry of Federico García Lorca, of course.

---

5   In the offending essay, which did not make the editorial cut, I made an offhand remark about "poetically gifted cows and shadowy figures like Braulio and Tasha, who some of you suspect may not exist outside of my imagination."

Deer hunters tell of season's success

Thanksgiving is past, and I'll wager that, over the holiday weekend, a fair number of you were out in the cold trying to shoot a deer before Sunday's close of another hunting season.

That season is now history. Either you got your deer or it eluded you. My congratulations or condolences, whichever are in order, go out to individual sportsmen (and women).

I already know that some of you had enjoyed early successes.

During bow season, for instance, Evan Park told me of shooting one from his back porch, beyond which his broken leg kept him from straying far. I and his classmates were glad that this season's bad fortune didn't extend to all aspects of his life.

Later, after rifle season had opened, Chris LeClere showed me snapshots of the one he'd bagged. If Chris were only as formidable in the Spanish classroom as he is in the woods, and on the football field and basketball court, I'm afraid I'd hardly be able to keep pace with him!

Others of my English students, this year and last, have managed to work their hunting experiences into various compositions. The best work I saw last year from Steve Ahl, for example, was an evocative description of the moments leading up to first sighting of a deer.

It was as good a work as any of his classmates contributed on that assignment. I don't think he'd known he had it in him.

This year Jeremy Conder, who at this writing is poised for a move from Perry County, writes passionately of his pursuit of an albino deer that got away from him.

In the teacher's lounge over lunch, Chris Seitz tells the tale of a friend who'd got a deer that was part albino. An expensive deer, it turns out, since, among other things, the lucky hunter was preparing to mount the head and have a rug made of its hide.

Chris was, himself, preparing for another go at the chase, hoping for his own success.

The albino chases, for their part, lend themselves to other meditations. I recall Greywolf's answer to a question at the library a few weeks back; yes, the albino has traditionally been viewed by Native American peoples as a sacred animal, the killing of which one doesn't take lightly.

However non-Indian hunters respond to this, a sense of sacredness would seem present in Jeremy's writing this year, and I imagine in Chris Seitz's friend's encounter with the animal whose memory he's going to such expense to preserve.

The responsible hunter knows that, however he interprets them, his relationship and responsibility to the natural world are sacred ones. Would that all buffalo slayers past and present were less careless of that truth.

That is a truth, I think, that Disney reflects in his feature-length cartoon, *Bambi*.

I know that some hunters will scoff at that, like a Bloomington sportswriter, some years back, complaining at anti-hunting opinion in the wake of Disney's re-release of that old classic. Were Disney more responsible to the truth, the writer suggested in that much-talked-about piece, he would have substituted the word "poachers" for "man."

The honest sportsman, the writer contended, would not have left the forest ablaze.

Fortunately, Disney didn't seek such counsel, which, whatever merits it might otherwise have, would have been death to *Bambi* as art, as well as to any overarching theme about man's place within the natural world.

Still, it's not necessary to sentimentalize the deer's plight, as is borne out by the following story.

My good friend Dean Dudley was just down from Bloomington so that our two families could share a turkey dinner. He told me of the rampant deer population up that way.

During previous winters, some of the non-hunting contingent had put out hay for the deers to eat; now they are upset that the increasing numbers of those animals are also eating carefully manicured flower gardens.

The upshot of it all is that the formerly maligned hunters of Monroe County are now acknowledged, by at least some of the Disney crowd, as good.

My gentle mom, who fortunately had no daughters to name Bambi, remains a possible exception.

A few comments to ease Mom's mind

I have to be fair to my mother.

You read last week, at the tail end of my piece on deer hunting, that my brothers and I give thanks for not having been born girls. Mom, enraptured by Disney's fairest fawn, had talked of making a namesake of her dreamed-of girl.

Now, I know that Bambi was a boy deer, but in human terms that name's translation is distinctly feminine. We also give thanks, then, that in the naming of one of us she didn't give in to that argument that Bambi was, after all, a boy deer.

I have to give Mom credit. She was kinder than Johnny Cash's pa, who the song says named him Sue.

Actually, as you may know, my name is Brett Alan.[6] I was named after a TV charmer and maverick played by James Garner, and a friend of my mom's who I don't really know but is probably still roaming around somewhere.

The next of three brothers, Todd Franklin, is named, first of all, for no one in particular, and second, for the line of Sanders men through John and Everett and Richard Franklin.

Kirk Regan, who I told you plans to be a classical philosopher if he ever grows up, was named after Captain Kirk of *Star Trek* fame or Kirk Douglas (take your pick) and, despite the loss of an *a*, Ronald Reagan, who became governor of California in the days we lived there.

We lived in Torrance, a suburb of LA, from my kindergarten through third-grade years.

I remember being present at a Reagan rally during that time, and breathing in my parents' enthusiasms for him at home.

That's another reason I should be fair to my mom.

Having just returned from a Thanksgiving in Austin, Texas, with Kirk, only to pick up the paper and read my political coming-out-of-the-closet, she's undoubtedly had all of the emotional upset she needs for a while.

With the three of us boys, she can never be sure what's next.

Brett abandoning worldly attachments and joining some ill-fated liberation movement in Latin America?

Todd hopping on a Harley Hogg and becoming a Hell's Angel?

Kirk appearing on *Larry King Live* and declaring as an enlightened dictator-for-life of the new, ultra-conservative Republic of Alaska?

It's in honest deference to all the pain and turmoil we've caused her that I publicly declare, then, for the perpetual rest and tranquility of her soul, that I am not now, nor have I ever been, nor am I likely to become a deer hunter.

My dad did take me squirrel hunting once, when I was five or six, and he helped me hold the gun for one shot.

He got another squirrel. I vaguely recall not liking the taste of it.

I remember his hunting some kind of bird, maybe pigeons, in Arizona, but after first leaving Perry County with my mom, Dad gradually ceased hunting, too — except, as he says, with a camera.

He'll still fish. The best picture I ever took of him is of him alone, fishing, at the base of a waterfall in upper Michigan.

We fished together in Alaska once, too, for salmon. I loved the eating, but the gentle nature toward animals that I'd imbibed from my mom caused me immeasurable suffering at the inevitable killing that came first.

I had to crush their skulls with a rock. I hit too softly. It killed me to see them writhe.

If I were to break down and go hunting with my new Perry County friends, I'm sure I'd be like Joel on *Northern Exposure*. Bagging the prey, finding the poor thing still breathing, I'd rush it into Tell City to see if the veterinarian could revive it.

I'm not apologizing for that part of my nature. It's a legacy from my mother that I willingly embrace.

I also try to be gentle to my fellow human creatures.

I figure the world's already a violent enough place without my small contribution to the mayhem.

---

6   To my newspaper readers, I was known simply as Brett Sanders.

1993: Talk of the County

Welcoming a new Yuletide kitten

If I even bothered to make new year's resolutions anymore, I'd resolve to be kind to my family's new Yuletide kitten in 1993.

Now, there's a promise I could keep without undue stress or perfectionist self-criticism.

Our new cat is a boy, a two-to-three-month-old tiger-yellow shorthair that I like to call Precioso, Spanish for his given name, Precious.

Precious comes to us as an early Christmas present, a surprise dividend from a recent trip to Bloomington. By now, he's a full-fledged member of the family, filling the place if not the memory of our first cat, Patches.

Precious is a playful and loving kitten, at ease with human company. He and I are already inseparable. He'll curl up on my lap and sleep. Awake, he'll chew my beard, lick my neck, and kiss my mouth.

People who say cats are not affectionate have just not understood them.

A cat's love may not be fawning like a dog's (I grew up with dogs and love them on their own terms), but it is love, nonetheless.

Cats, in this respect, have been given a bum rap. That's the argument of Warren and Fay Eckstein, anyway, in their book called *How to Get Your Cat to Do What You Want.*

"Any pet is a product of what's put into him or her," the Ecksteins write.

"Because we have been brainwashed into thinking that cats are independent, aloof, sometimes less affectionate and certainly less trainable, many cat owners treat their cats differently just because they're cats!"

In fact, as a subtitle in the book proclaims, the Ecksteins think that cats are actually so smart that "they've convinced people they can't be trained!"

The cat, in any case, has surely been created for our benefit and companionship, and I have felt this love.

A story from the book *Cat Tales*, with photographs by Robin Upward and an introduction by Cleveland Amory, tells of a magician who rewarded the good Samaritan who'd come to his aid by creating the first Persian cat out of a handful of smoke, a flame, and two bright stars.

"Take it home," the magician said. "It will be a plaything for thy children and an ornament to thy house."

Indeed, a good cat is all of that, and if cultivated as a friend, as good a one as any dog.

True stories are legion, but here is my favorite.

A mother, visiting the room of the daughter she'd just disciplined, finds there two wet pillows and sets of eyes, the child's and her cat's.

Incidents of cats' learning to do things we think they wouldn't be caught dead doing are also not uncommon.

James Herriot, beloved veterinarian and writer, tells in his picture-story book, *The Christmas Day Kitten*, of a cat that even chases and retrieves a rubber ball, while the lazy dogs sit and watch.

So why not walk on a leash? Or stop scratching the furniture?

You can't teach a cat not to scratch, the Ecksteins admit, but you can teach them what to scratch.

As you are imperfect, so will your cat be sometimes, neglecting to do everything you want all of the time, but as the

Ecksteins also say, "part of the joy of having a cat is being around a free thinker."

Not a robot, but "an intelligent and loving member of the family."

The language that performs that miracle? Just call it love, the same magic that must have given us cats in the first place, and that continues to work for most other animals and even some people.

Christmas in Texas and Argentina

As Bing Crosby dreams once more of a white Christmas, my mind goes back to a couple of other Christmases in my past.

One took place in Argentina, the other in Texas. Neither was particularly white.

Christmas in Houston was cold, I'll give it that. My parents and brother, traveling by van to share it with us, were fortunate to make it at all. They fought an ice storm west through Arkansas and south through eastern Texas.

The visiting with family was a joyous gift, anyway, for one as depressed as I was after a semester in Hell, a.k.a. Alexander Hamilton Middle School.

Yet it was within the walls of that school, with the children whose lives I had hoped to touch more dramatically than I possibly could, that I experienced the Christmas that I most treasure from that city.

The best gift came out of my hardest class, a section of English as a Second Language populated by over thirty Mexican-American seventh graders, most of whom seemed intent on my and my lessons' destruction.

Leticia Ortiz was intensely studying the instructions on the board when I discovered the gift-wrapped surprise on my desk. She alone in the class, then, as was her daily custom, began work on the assignment.

The present was a tiny ball of fur that her note said was a koala bear, plus a cheap plastic rosary and other knick-knacks.

Her note said that I was a special teacher. Like any child of mortal parents, a teacher stands in need, sometimes, of such affirming words.

My first Christmas on the Argentine pampa was different. It came in the dead of summer, not a month after my arrival there. The sun was hot.

For Christmas Eve, my Californian missionary companion and I were invited to a farm on the outskirts of the next town.

I only have space to briefly sketch the scene.

Little girls twirling around in the twilight and the growing dark, dancing to the scratchy waltzes from the old phonograph outside the long, L-shaped adobe house.

Firecrackers exploding at midnight, neighbors descending with hugs and kisses for everyone.

Delighted children running around and shouting after the three kings' secretive visit, each one with his or her toy. (That's one less stop that Santa has to make.)

Men in the open pit preparing the roast for the midnight feast. Everyone dancing afterward under Christmas morning stars.

My partner and I, having missed the bus home, spent the night in the local church.

I still wish I'd followed that Californian's relaxed example, putting aside mission rules just that once and dancing with the pretty teenage girl who'd invited me.

I was barely twenty years old. It was a painful sacrifice.

Strangely enough, though, that first Christmas away from home, without even a hint of snow, was on the whole not painful at all. It was beautiful. Warm. Full of love.

Houston had its share of love, too, the sometimes-innocence of those who have little else to give.

A white Perry County Christmas would be nice, but a change for Christmas, a multi-cultural surprise, as it were, can go a long way.

To wander or not: Listen to the spirits

A few random thoughts in favor of roaming.

And of staying put.

First, a conversation with Robert Bryant, itinerant teacher and musician, known hereabouts as Hoosier Bob. Feeling fine, he says, after recent knee and hip surgery.

Among other important matters we discussed recently were our separate beginnings in journalism, particularly his renewed urge to get back into photojournalism. And to the road.

I can understand that urge. I love to go places, too. I almost envied my fellow teacher, last June's roommate in the Yucatán, for his wistful remembering of a bike trip down the Interamerican Highway to Argentina.

He took a plane back from the top of the continent.

~*~

To be rooted in a place, as I and Hoosier Bob are in Perry County, can be good.

My family's future is in this place, rooted in my larger family's past.

The Kroessmans came with the original Swiss colonizers. Mary Kroessman, my mom's mom, was born and raised around here. She spoke German before she spoke English. The schools here, before she attended them, were once bilingual.

That German-English bilingualism has nourished my own English-Spanish bilingualism. In turn, I try to nourish the linguistic heritage of a few area students.

~*~

Indiana writer Scott Sanders (no relation), in an essay excerpted in the January / February 1993 issue of the *Utne Reader*, speaks eloquently of staying put.

"I cannot have a spiritual center without having a geographic one," he writes.

But, won't staying put make him parochial?

"I've met ignorant people who have never moved," he writes; "and I have also met ignorant people who never stood still."

The sacred spot, then, is within, wherever we settle or wander.

"You know," he quotes a Native American holy man as saying, "I think if people stay somewhere long enough — even white people — the spirits will begin to speak to them. The spirits and the old powers aren't lost, they just need people to be around long enough and the spirits will begin to influence them."

~*~

Every people has a story to tell, my good neighbor Greywolf observes. Likewise, we all have old powers and spirits that are willing to influence us.

The spirits of our own people and of our religious traditions. I am as sure of this as of anything else.

At the first of the new year I was up north with Anita, way out in the country southeast of Bedford and the little village of Budda (the *h* is vanished).

We traversed the splendid geography of the Devil's Backbone, as it is known thereabouts, a jutting, meandering spine of land looking down on golden valleys.

Our friends' wedding was held in the historical Dixon Chapel. No electric lights or heat, but a wood-burning stove. Beautiful white wooden structure.

The bride and groom, listening to the spirits that tie them to places both near and far — and to old but still living traditions — were dressed in a combination of folksy European and Elizabethan Renaissance attire.

The moment was simple and holy. The vows our friends shared echoed the most sacred rites and Davidic psalms.

If you listened quietly enough you heard the spirits, too.

Not so different, really, from the ones we might notice hereabouts where, with Hoosier Bob and all the rest of you, I am still glad to make my home.

Confabulating with the cows and walking leashed cats

Some of my students would probably say that I'm about the funniest thing to come along since Rowan and Martin's *Laugh-In* — that is, if only their collective memory went back that far, and if I weren't a boring language teacher.

First there's all that silly talk, as they foolishly call it, about confabulating cows, one of the invisible realities of God's creation that, according to the first chapter of the apostle Paul's epistle to the Romans, are "clearly seen" (or heard) by those who are initiated into the secrets.

"What's this I'm hearing about you?" Bill Bockstahler bellowed one day as he walked into the teacher's lounge. (I was grading papers. He headed for the photocopier.)

"What do you mean?" I queried.

"About talking cows!" he said. "My students are saying you talk to cows, and they talk back to you or something."

"That's true," I said, responding in equally confident tones. "Absolutely true."

It seems that Tammy Madden had been repeating the tale, wonderingly recounting some of my recent ravings. In case the students don't all read the paper, you know — I want to be sure they're informed.

(Bockstahler, for his part, hailing from Dubois County as he does, was bound to have missed it.)

Then there's the rumor that I've actually been seen in my front yard with a leashed cat.

"Leashes are for dogs!" they shout, all seventeen in that Spanish class rolling on the floor in hysterical laughter.

"You're crazy!" they add for good measure, and, "Oh, I read in the paper the other day where you wrote about your cat."

That was Jamie George, whose granddad lives across the street from us and once loaned me a ladder.

Andy Sommer, cheerful cat owner himself, I take it, said, "You have a house cat?" To my, "*Sí, señor,*" he answered, "All right!" Still, the idea of a cat on a leash struck everyone as about as insane an idea as my conversing with cows.

"Very interesting!" they might have said, echoing Arte Johnson's famous *Laugh-In* character.

"Have you seen a psychiatrist?"

Well, I'll stick by my story, anyway, with the apostle Paul as my backup. And, as far as the leash goes, the Ecksteins (whom I quoted in that other piece about cats) — *say* I can walk my cat on a leash.

So there!

If only Jamie could have seen me the other day, though, as I ran across to her grandpa's barn (he wasn't home) to borrow his ladder again.

This time it was to get the cat out of a neighbor's tree. Precious had gotten away from Stephanie, who had been walking him for me.

The tree was tall. The cat kept going higher, the leash slowing his movements and, as it got tangled up in the branches, making them more dangerous.

Conscious of my daughter's tears and the prospect of becoming a hero, I climbed James George's ladder and saved our cat, who was climbing further out on a limb but came back toward the sound of my voice. I reached out to untangle the leash, then took Precious with one hand and started down.

Inside the house, his heart was racing. Perhaps he was thinking of his close scrape with death.

I still insist that leashes can be an advantage, but admittedly not in every circumstance.

If the vision of me and my cat in a tree doesn't make Jamie laugh, anyway, here's a story Bill Wilkins told me when I'd finished relating to him Precious's Big Adventure.

He told of a little baby goat he and the family had once owned, and of tying it to a tree so it wouldn't get loose. Unfortunately for the poor kid, they tied it to a high branch instead of to the trunk. The kid, circling the tree several times, ended up dangling upright just off the ground, where in the morning they found it about as dead as a doornail. As my cat almost did, it had hung itself.

Have you ever heard a more pathetic story?

"Should you ever be drowned or hung," says Stephen King's artistic forebear Edgar Allan Poe, "be sure and make a note of your sensations."

I don't know whether to laugh or cry.

Snow: If you can't beat it, enjoy it!

These February snow storms (March, at this writing, is just around the corner) have put me in mind of winters past.

First I think of the (in)famous Blizzard of '78, which caused the cancellation of classes at IU-Bloomington for the first time in the history of that university. I was a freshman there that year, and, in any case, could not have made it in to campus from my parents' home outside of Ellettsville.

That winter, with its sub-zero temperatures, record snowfall, and national coal strike, was certainly one to remember, but so was the winter before that. I was co-editor then of the Bloomington daily's weekly youth supplement. A January 18 report of mine from Edgewood High School reminds me that we'd already had five snow days, which, at the time, state law did not require to be made up.

I had no complaints about that, to be sure!

At about the same time, Joe Aaron was writing about snow for the *Evansville Courier*, where some of my readers will remember having read his "Morning Assignment" for many years. This particular column was clipped by my grandma Mary Kroessman, who was kind enough to pass it on to me.

It seems that "on the occasion of our first snowfall of the winter," as he explained it, he had "composed an unrestrained song of praise — and of thanksgiving, too, and of childlike exultation — to its clean, white beauty."

Since then, he'd been held personally accountable, by fans who didn't share that enthusiasm, "for every car that would not start, for every whining tire that could not get a grip on an icy pavement, for every furnace that expired in the frozen stretches of the night and every water line that busted."

He added, "It's all my fault, don't you see — every miserable tatter of it — and my popularity, once a thing to write home about, has all but ceased to exist."

He made a good defense, anyway, and come fair weather was undoubtedly forgiven, as I hope I will be, though I confess to being delighted in the snow as much as Joe Aaron was.

The recent weather, as I said, has prompted a lot of memories, and a recent drive out of Indianapolis toward Bloomington, a couple of hours into our second big snow storm in as many weeks, was a moment of pleasure rather than of any nervousness on my part.

I drove slowly, and I recalled those old times while listening to a combination of jazz, blues, and traditional pop on Butler and Indiana University radio stations.

I remembered, for instance, from the early Eighties when I'd been a young married student, the pleasing crunch of snow under the tires of my old yellow Volkswagen Beetle as I made my rounds delivering pizza.

I also remembered losing my keys in a snowdrift at two in the morning one night soon after Jonathan was born.

I had to walk the distance to the hospital to wake Anita up for her keys so I could get into the trailer and sleep. My own keys turned up a day or two later, thanks to the nice person who found them near where I'd parked, and tracked me down by the number on the trailer key.

Both of these memories, and others like them, feel good as I take hold of them once again and try them on for size.

I think that the purity of freshly fallen snow appeals to an inner sense of ours that longs to snatch beauty out of even the most beastly of experiences.

Few people cherish the extreme cold or other hardships, even death, that winter may bring, but a fresh blanket of snow on the ground is surely a beautiful antidote to the drabness that so often engulfs us for months on end.

If we can't prevent it from happening (and let's face it: you can't stop Mother Nature any more than I can force her), then we may as well allow our spirits to enjoy, if only from behind a window, its clean beauty.

If it does snow again, (and who knows? perhaps by the time you read this it will have), I'll probably be right there where Joe Aaron was before me, "my nose pressed to the window, grinning happily like a little kid with a new sled."

Thanks, by the way, to the Good Samaritan neighbor (Anita thinks it was Larry James behind the ski mask) who, last time it snowed, cleared out our driveway for us while I was gone.

I had been conducting business in Bloomington after a teacher's workshop the previous day in Indianapolis. I came back to Perry County that Saturday morning, two days after the snow, which was still thick on the ground and bright against a blue sky and radiant sun.

Don Quixote: Tilting at windmills in Kentuckiana

I was off to Louisville the other day for one more proverbial tilt at the windmills.

The occasion was an educational, bilingual production of *"Las Aventuras de Don Quixote de La Mancha."* I was accompanied by my own children and a group of my students.

The story is adapted to the stage from Miguel de Cervantes's famous novel of late 16th-, early 17th-century Spain. It involves a knight, his trusty squire-assistant, and their strange adventures together.

The knight — really, he's an idealistic old gentleman who, rechristening himself Don Quixote, assumes the role of a knight-errant — sets off from his home region of La Mancha to seek adventures and to restore Spain to her abandoned code of chivalry, defending right and honor in a dishonorable world.

Donkey Hotay, we often call him, ignoring that the "Don" is not a name at all but his appropriated title of nobility, comparable to the British "Sir," and with a long *o* instead of an *ah*.

Sancho Panza, his squire, is a practical-minded but simple peasant who, while hoping fancifully for riches and honors, has his feet firmly planted on the ground, where he tries to keep his master's.

The most famous of their adventures involves Don Quixote's attacking a bunch of windmills that he takes for giants. Hence the phrase "tilting at windmills." Tilting, or jousting, refers to the ancient sport of running at an opponent with a lance — on horseback, of course.

It was fun to see that adventure acted out onstage (without the horse). The whole play, for that matter, was a delight to watch, despite the acoustics that occasionally muddled up some dialogue.

The most innovative aspect of the staging involves a reversing of a scene in order to play it back in the other language. It's done like this: the action freezes, the stage goes dark, and then the actors go backwards, partially, through the just completed scenes, strobe lights playing off of their movements.

The effect is dazzling, sort of a combination of rock video staccato and silent film played in reverse.

The silent film analogy is a happy one. I have often thought that Chaplin's beloved Tramp, at once absurd and sublime, is a lot like Don Quixote. There's more to each than meets the eye.

Sancho, too, is no mere bumpkin or clown. He's a clever fellow, good Sancho, and he changes his master as surely as he is changed by him — into a practical-minded peasant with a fresh touch of idealism.

Don Quixote, for his part, is gradually persuaded of the wisdom of certain of Sancho's precautions regarding their mortality.

In the end, he dies brokenhearted, renouncing all of his deeds as pure madness, telling his protesting squire — who yearns for more adventures with his master — that you can't change the whole world.

In point of truth, though, Don Quixote had changed his world in some small degree, as he continues to do so today across space and time.

As we "dream the impossible dream" (a line from the American musical *Man of La Mancha*, inspired by Cervantes's character), we dream our knight's dream of a world where our own and our fellows' dignity is mutually valued, protected, cherished.

It is true that Don Quixote's peculiar adventures have come to symbolize ill-conceived ventures of all sorts: "there goes another fool, fighting with the windmills of his imagination." We call these adventures *quixotic* [quick-SAH-tick], by which we mean foolish, even laughable.

But is it madness to strike out against the insane rationality of a depraved world, which Don Quixote does, albeit misguidedly by trying to revive a fictitious order of chivalry?

I first made Don Quixote's acquaintance when I was fifteen, and I knew then as I know now that he was no mere fool.

I saw the giants, too, and would perhaps have chased them, myself.

Reality is a multi-leveled experience, and there is, indeed, more to it than meets the eye.

Truth is concealed — sometimes, at least — beneath the surface of an absurdity.

Timely reminder of democratic principles

I met Braulio and Tasha the other night for the opening of the Perry Central musical production of *The Sound of Music*.

They were as delighted as I and the family.

"Kate Seibert," (who my daughter Stephanie idolizes), "is the definitive Maria," Tasha exclaimed. "Why, she almost puts Julie Andrews to shame!"

"And Matt Archibald," Braulio added, "is a fair rival to that bloke who played opposite Andrews in the movie."

And there were other whispers, too, about Emily Krueger's precocious smile, Jeremi Morris's engaging voice, Stephanie Hagman as a truly "wicked" Mother Superior, and on and on . . . (if I go any further, I'm afraid I'll leave somebody out, and I really think that the whole performance was too good for words).

Most of our conversation, though, after we'd gotten through with those niceties, revolved around the meatier issues of democracy, freedom, prejudice, and oppression that the play gets at in its still-entertaining format.

Both of my friends were visibly moved by the emotion of the last segments, with Jeremy Hay raising his swastika-banded arm and shouting, *"Heil, Hitler!"* and the Von Trapps making their way toward the Swiss Alps and freedom from Nazi tyranny.

"Freedom is something that you Americans don't value as deeply as you think you do," Tasha said, memories of her pre-defection travail in Soviet Russia fresh in her mind.

And Braulio, who, not so long ago, could not walk around in his native city of Buenos Aires without fear of the death squads, tended to agree.

"Witness all the unfair criticism you get for the liberal pronouncements in some of your columns," he said. "Democracy is not neat and tidy, where opposing people and ideas are just put out of the way."

I did have to admit that I'd received a bit of cranky mail recently, critical of my support of that "baby killer" in the White House, but I was quick to point out to my friends that most of the ribbing I take has been all in good fun.

Paul Seibert, for example, in company with other teachers and family, accused me of being a liberal and of thus (my sleeves alone were turned down in the cool of the evening) not believing in "baring arms."

Just to prove my mettle, and to demonstrate that I can bare my arms with the best of them, I proceeded to roll up my sleeves. I may be a liberal, but I can be as stupidly macho as the next guy.

Tasha and Braulio have valid points, though, and I had to concur with them on the larger ones.

I, too, have been troubled lately by the hate climate that has seemed increasingly evident in the wake of the conservative 80's, when the watchwords, on at least one level, became law and order and property rights at the expense of the Jeffersonian civil liberties that we depend on to keep from Germany's and Argentina's and Soviet Russia's mistakes of oppression.

"The scapegoating is still there in your economic paranoia," Tasha said, "and that's the issue that gave Hitler his power."

"And your marching Klansmen and skinheads, in the name of law and order and racial and ideological purity, are also not unlike the bigots who terrorized my republic," Braulio added.

As far as the liberal bent of some of my election and inaugural season essays, I must point out, myself, that the particulars of my liberalism are similar to the turn-of-the-century progressivism that typified Republican hero and rough rider Theodore Roosevelt. A man may be both liberal and conservative.

The titles as used are often meaningless, and, in any case, I only expressed "tentative" support for that guy who I helped elect in November, who, for the sake of popularity, is as law-and-order as the candidate I more deliberately repudiated, and who already has reneged on some significant campaign promises.

Somewhere else, I might be able to give a sensible defense of a certain type of liberalism, as distinct from Republican or Democratic party ideology, but here there's only space to say this: I do value freedom, and, if not another's, then how my own?

Democracy is a messy business sometimes, but it beats the alternatives. Thanks to the Perry Central singers and actors for a timely reminder.

Huckleberry Finn: A study
of inner religious struggle

Since Disney's sweetly sentimentalized *Huck Finn* has surely, by this reading, run its course at the local cinema, I guess it's safe for me to say that it was rather a disappointment to me and the family.

It was no match for Roger Miller's Broadway musical success of *Big River*, which we saw last summer at Lincoln City, and which captured, if not all the detail of the novel, all the essence of its spirit and language.

Certainly it was no match either for Mark Twain's original, which British writer Arthur Henry King calls "one of the most moral books ever written."

"*Huckleberry Finn* has religious depth," King continues, "and one sees that Twain must have been struggling against that religious depth in himself all his life. That is why he produced superficiality from time to time."

In another moment — I can't turn up the exact quotation at this writing — King refers to one of those superficialities in the personage of Tom Sawyer, whose playful manipulation of his fellow beings, as exemplified in the famous incident of the whitewashed fence, is supremely inhumane, despite what King observes as our puzzling American tendency to glorify such inhumanities ("Boys will be boys . . .").

Tom Sawyer's games, whose outcomes have no moral significance at all, are the antithesis of the deadly serious game that Huck and his runaway slave Jim are compelled to play for the dignity and freedom that Tom and his society thoughtlessly enjoy.

Perhaps one of the Disney version's principal faults is that Tom is, for the most part, so noticeably absent, because as much as his pranks irritate us within the seriousness of this novel, we need them, along with the duke and king's grotesque deceptions, to stand against Huck's deeper moral dilemma and to sharpen that dilemma for us.

In keeping with this artistic problem of Tom's absence is the fact that Disney's Huck is a darling boy (who ever pictured Twain's Huck like that?) who is not meant, by his creators, to be wholly distinguishable from the idealized Tom whose imaginative adventures are immortalized in Magic Kingdoms from Los Angeles to Orlando.

Disney's Jim, too, is Hollywood picture perfect, no match for the rough grace that one reads into Twain's character.

This rough grace in Twain's great American novel — unsweetened, unsentimentalized — is the essence of the book's religious character.

Speaking of a vision of heaven painted for him by smugly religious Widow Douglas and Miss Watson — a place where all you do is float on a cloud and play a harp — Huck observes: "Well, I couldn't seen no advantage in going where she was going, so I made up my mind I wouldn't try for it. But I never said so, because it would only make trouble, and wouldn't do no good."

He believes in that heaven, though, and in the social code of right and wrong that hides behind its pseudo-religious cloak.

This is the book's terrible irony: that Huck imagines he'll go to Hell (nevertheless choosing to risk it) for helping a good, decent man to run away from the society that immorally presumes to own and sell him.

Huck, without knowing it, is the truly religious figure at story's center.

His struggle with comfortable religiosity mirrors some of my own inner struggles with organized religion grown secure in its righteousness, whether it be reflected in my own honored tradition and faith or in someone else's.

I begin to sympathize, then, with naive, simple, honest Huck, who, in the good slave Jim's words is, "de bes' friend Jim's ever had . . . de on'y white genlman dat ever kep' his promise to ole Jim."

And with Honest Abe Lincoln, who, among so many other things, said this:

"When any church will inscribe over its altar, as its sole qualification for membership, the Savior's condensed statement of the substance of both law and Gospel, 'Thou shalt love thy God with all thy heart and with all thy soul, and thy neighbor as thyself,' that church will I join with all my heart and all my soul."

On the "wicked" good fun of wordplay . . .

I had a call the other day from an interested reader with an interesting question about a particular adjective I'd tossed out in that week's column.

He got me thinking. I'm afraid he may have thought, by the way I was slipping into the privacy of those thoughts of mine, that I didn't value his contribution to them. I hope through these words to rectify the unintended wrong.

The question, in the first place, was good: whatever did I mean by referring to Stephanie Hagman as a "wicked" Mother Superior in the student production of *The Sound of Music*? The role, after all, was if anything compassionate, and that's how Stephanie played it.

My immediate response was that I'd not meant for the word to be taken quite so literally — that's why I put it in quotation marks — but to reflect a usage I have occasionally heard from the kids themselves, wherein bad means good, and wicked, superb.

"You took the word too seriously," I said, not meaning any insult. "I was just playing."

You've heard of an athlete having a wicked backhand, for instance, the connotation suggesting expertness more than strict evil.

I have also heard a girl ask something like, "How do you like my new hairstyle?" and be answered with a thoroughly approving and enthusiastic "Wicked!"

Yet there's more that should have been said to my questioner, if I'd let the conversation play out more fully, because my mind was just beginning to turn over some of the less apparent, perhaps even subconscious, levels of the wordplay.

I went to my *Webster's* after we'd hung up, leaving the dishwater to sit for a moment. I found there a secondary meaning of the word ("mischievous, roguish, 'a wicked grin'") that seemed to suggest another motive to my employing it.

Would Stephanie's mom or dad, or her classmates or teachers, think me rude if I confessed to having detected, once or twice, a wickedly mischievous grin about her?

I am remembering the April coffeehouse, and a young fellow's teasing remark about our especially spiritual nuns who, with the others of the cast, were about to sing. The playfulness in his words reflected the girls' flowing hair (no religious habits that night) and our knowledge of them as fun-loving teenagers, not ready in real life for the convent.

"Oh, you'd make a lovely Mother Superior!" a parent teases Stephanie after a performance. She has other ideas, though, and is free in saying so.

I suppose I was drawing on all of that when I confused dozens of my readers with that mischievous adjective.

. . . and the exotic art of ostrich farming

Sabine Vollmer's recent "Lifestyle" piece on an effort in Perry County to farm Argentine ostriches [or, rheas] found a fascinated reader in me.

To Dale and Rosa Brown, the rhea farmers, whose son Matthew is my son Jonathan's schoolmate, I proclaim my sincerest best wishes for success.

I've long considered, since coming back to the States and reading such pampean masterpieces as Lucio Mansilla's *Excursion to the Ranquel Indians* (which I'm engaged in translating), that a glaring hole in my own experience down that way is that I never saw, in its natural environment, a live rhea, or guanaco, or any one of a million species of armadillo of which he writes.

Since then, passing between Indiana and Texas in a blur of automotive speed, I've caught the hint of a dead armadillo or two along Arkansas highways, but somehow that's less than I'd hoped for.

Who knew that, for a live South American specimen, I'd have to look no further than home? Farmed birds may not be the same as wild ones hunted on the prairie, caught with a throw of the gaucho's *bolas*, but they're something. This summer when I come back to Mansilla I'll have to look St. Croix-way for inspiration.

The *bolas*, if you don't know, are a set of three stones, usually rounded and wrapped in rawhide, tied to a large rope like a lariat. The Argentine cowboy, or gaucho, throws them at the feet of the animal he's chasing, thus tripping it up to where he can jump off his horse and subdue it.

The *bolas* are a gift from the pampean, or prairie, Indians, who, for their favor, the conquering Spaniards exterminated, much as we did a large percentage of our North American Indians. This annihilation of a people, which Mansilla almost alone among his compatriots resists, is the central material of his book that also puts me in mind of ostriches.

He begins the book, which consists of a series of letters published first in serial form in a newspaper, by mentioning the choice experience of eating an ostrich-egg omelet at Nagüel Mapo, among the Indians he sought to parley with. Of "touching once again," as he comments to his friend and public, "life's extremes."

The Browns, departing from the mundane realities of pig and cow farming (please don't imagine that I belittle pig or cow farmers!), have touched life's extremes through the risk they've taken, and inspired this humble writer in the process.

At this point, I must mention an agricultural scheme of my own, which, given the facts of our Perry County climate, might have to be pulled off somewhere else.

Picture, if you will, growing iguanas, a culinary product whose cultivation both tickles the palate (tastes like chicken, I'm told, as every beast and its cousin claims to) and saves endangered jungle from encroaching cattle.

I read a few years back, in the *Christian Science Monitor*, of such ventures in the semi-tropics of Central America, and wrote a whimsical paragraph about that newspaper's gentle founder, Mary Baker Eddy, riding off into the Costa Rican jungle "astride a giant reptile."

"She is crusading for the preservation of rainforests," I write, "cultivating iguanas like chickens, or cattle, scattering new trees behind her. I half determine, if vanquished by Orwellian realities, to become an iguana farmer."

Now that there is a family of rhea farmers right here at home, I won't have to go to such extremes to get away from the nervous stress of the classroom.

Thanks go out to Sabine from Anita for stopping me short the other day, just as my iguana-farming bags were packed.

I also enjoyed Sabine's opinion piece (I didn't realize she was European) on the controversial Swiss book with its not-so-rosy view of Tell City. A little inward glance never hurt anyone. It's only the failure to recognize our shortcomings and to constructively meet them that stunts our growth.[7]

---

7   My decade-long, off and on translation of Mansilla's book came up short when I discovered two English translations published in that year of 1997. But the end result was a series of correspondences that led to my successful publication — all connected, in one way or another, to Mansilla's book and that Indian frontier — of an original novella and, in translation from the Spanish, of a book of prose poetry and a novel by Buenos Aires writer María Rosa Lojo.

More harmony than the law allows?

Those of us who witnessed the doings at the coffee house a couple of Fridays past might well have considered our weekend complete before it had even begun.

What more could we ask than Tell City's venerable Dixie Davis on piano, accompanied by a feisty jazz combo featuring, among others whose names I don't recall, Floyd Freeman (that supposedly irascible school board member) on trumpet?

That was enough for me, but then we had a Lincoln Boyhood storyteller, a younger local talent with a revisionist history (in verse) of the Cinderella story, and a potpourri of other musicians and singers. "More fun," as the radio line goes, "than the law allows."

That should have been enough, as I said, but of course it wasn't. Fortunately, the family and I were invited to Saturday evening's festivities across the highway from us, over at the pond between Larry Fleming's new house and his father-in-law, Paul Wilkins's, newer one, both of which are the handiwork of Bernie Bower.

Paul Wilkins, as many of you will know, heads up a country band that's been heard around these parts before, and Larry plays and sings with him, too. This was my first time to hear either of them, and they were joined on the Flemings' back porch by a motley crew of visitors, some of whom had never played with Paul before and had come from as far away as the Indianapolis area.

They were good. Paul, my student Lesly's dad, is a whale of
an entertaining guy who seems to have a whale of a good time as
he's entertaining.

He flashes a playful gleam of a smile as his head
waves sideways to the beat, keeping time and keeping up an
unspoken, teasing dialogue with the audience. His wide-brimmed
straw hat successfully disguises a pleasantly bald head
until he removes hat and mops head dry with a colorful
handkerchief, grinning all the while as he gets himself and his
crew set to play another number.

Ask him to play that mischievous little tune about the
education he got out behind his dad's barn. Otherwise there
are always the "dribbly" songs he likes to throw in to get you
all choked up, and a bunch of old country standards of every
variety.

My own Anita went up later in the evening and introduced
the two Stan LaGrange numbers with which she's auditioning in
Nashville on June 24. It seemed to me, and to the enthusiastic
crowd who cheered her, that she done pretty good for herself,
mostly.

Then I went up and sang a couple of songs in Spanish,
just so folks will keep thinking I don't know how to sing in
English.

"Was that country?" a friendly heckler asked me after the
first one.

"Not this country," I answered, and started strumming out
the second one on Paul's acoustic guitar.

My student hosts for this shindig were Lesly Wilkins
and her nephew and niece Karl and Gena Fleming. Also,
there was another of my students and Lesly's nephew,
William Tinch, who in the afternoon sun was burnt about as red
as a lobster.

It was nice to see all of them outside of school, and to enjoy
the beautiful setting and the relaxed company and good food.
Folks were two-stepping and slow-dancing around on grass and

straw, and kids were swimming and alternately rowing and sinking in a little boat. Some of us, too, were just heading back to the trough and eating more than we really had need of eating.

Paul and his crew should think of gracing our ears again with a little music sometime at the coffee house.

Dixie and Floyd and the jazz combo, too: they deserve a whole concert, and maybe the improvised harmonies of that trumpet and band will inspire Floyd and all the folks who've been quarreling with each other about the big town's schools to recognize their shared humanity and start resolving some old problems.

We can always hope, anyway. Nothing's a sweeter, shared language than music.

A flower that launched a thousand songs

I've been thinking lately of a charming little story called *The Little Prince*, by French writer and airplane pilot Antoine de Saint-Exupéry.

This is a wise little parable, a fable intended for children and discerning adults, for whoever has ears and eyes and heart to understand its wisdom.

Its narrator tells of being stranded, because of his plane's mechanical failure, in the midst of North Africa's Sahara Desert. While there, he meets a mysterious little prince, who'd come from a curiously tiny planet where he loved a single flower that was unique in all the world.

"Oh!" the little prince cried when he first saw her bloom. "How beautiful you are!"

"Am I not?" the flower responded sweetly. "And I was born at the same moment as the sun. . . ."

While she was none too modest, then, and quite flirtatious, she was also moving, and very exciting to the little prince. Still, she was carried away by her vanity, such as when, speaking of her four thorns, she exclaimed, "Let the tigers come with their claws!"

There were no tigers on the little prince's planet, and her tiny thorns would have been useless against them, anyway. She also spoke carelessly in other ways, until finally he lost confidence in her words and began to doubt her.

We learn in the rest of the fable, as the narrator learns, of how the little prince wanders away from his flower on a journey through other planets, and of how he sorts out from those experiences the wisdom that lies at the heart of all deeply felt relationships, and of how he at last returns to her.

Those of us who are most blessed have had a flower, too, which to us has been unique in all the world.

During the past school year, for instance, I kept at my desk a photograph of Anita, posing among other flowers at the United Nations rose garden in New York City.

That is probably my favorite picture of her, followed, I guess, by the one of her singing (long before we'd met) in a long pink dress and brown hair flowing past her shoulders.

Of course, I've never strayed as far as the little prince did, even though the initial romance, as is bound to happen in any relationship, has occasionally been strained.

The little prince, anyway, torn by his flower's absence, speaks regretfully of his hasty departure.

"The fact is," he says, "I did not know how I loved her! I ought to have judged by deeds and not by words. She cast her fragrance and her radiance over me. . . . I ought to have guessed all the affection that lay behind her little stratagems. . . ."

Later, he explains the wisdom gained by his having tamed (or been tamed by) the little fox he'd met on earth, the same fox who taught him why his flower, which he'd learned was just a common rose, after all, was still unique in all the world.

"What is important," the clever fox says, "is invisible to the eye.

"It is the time you have wasted for your rose that makes your rose so important.

"Man has forgotten this truth. . . . You become responsible, forever, for what you have tamed. You are responsible for your rose."

Responsibility, then, as it always must, has supplanted romance, though not totally. The excitement may remain, but in muted, matured form. What feverish youth cannot yet understand is that real loving requires work, maybe even the hardest work of which living beings are capable.

So it has proven to be with me and Anita. She cast her song and her radiance over me, and now we are responsible for each other, though as different from each other as the little prince from his flower.

Still she casts her song, though, as that fabled rose its fragrance. This week, as some of you know, she casts it the whole distance to Tennessee.

May that song be lifted up at the same moment as the sun that rises above it.

On Boone, respect, and burial grounds

As we were listening to Larry Whitman's soothing guitar over at the Franklin School the other night, my friend Greywolf and I exchanged a few words.

Greywolf's whole family had just performed with story, song, and dance, and would perform again.

In one of those moments, he told the traditional story of a daughter-in-law who learned, from her unkindness to her child's grandfather, the value of having him around, and of respecting his old ways and their wisdom.

As Greywolf and I chatted alone for this other moment, he remarked on how good it was that this old building, too, had not been forgotten, as so often buildings like it are torn down too hastily.

I had told him that my mom used to go to school there, walking from her house across the street, where her mother still lives.

My great-grandpa's name is engraved on the stone beside the school's entranceway, he having been one of the trustees at the time of its construction.

It was in the woods between the schoolyard and 9th Street that with my dad, back in the old days when boys were men, I would go tiger hunting, and we never came back without one.

Then, safely across the street in the safety of Grandma's house, Grandpa would bounce me on his knee and tell me stories of the even older, wilder days when he had used to go hunting in the Kentucky wilderness with Daniel Boone.

Now, some of my students don't believe that my grandpa hunted with Daniel Boone.

That's what he told me, though, and I know my grandpa was an honest man.

I'll just have to borrow a line from Oglala Sioux wise man Black Elk, who, upon relating one of the sacred stories, said: "This they tell, and whether it happened so or not I do not know; but if you think about it, you can see that it is all true."

My grandpa's Boone is also true, you see. The truth of some stories has little to do with whether it really happened.

Recently, anyway, I had read a 1992 Boone biography by John Mack Faragher, entitled *Daniel Boone: The Life and Legend of an American Pioneer*.

Boone was born in Pennsylvania in 1734 and died in Missouri in 1820. That is somewhat before my grandpa's chronological time, but who's to say that spirits don't travel, that we only live in one time frame?

The book, in any case, sheds some important light on the subject, and it seems to me (I haven't space to tell here of my own transhistorical interviews with the old frontiersman) that Boone felt he'd been treated rather fairly this time.

For instance, Faragher points out that, contrary to the Fess Parker image I grew up on and that my grandpa humored in me, Boone never in his life was a wearer of coonskin caps, nor was he a killer of Indians.

Davy Crockett was both of those things. He and Boone have been mixed up in the popular imagination.

Much of Boone's trouble in life came from two qualities: he lacked a killer instinct in business and was thus often in debt, and he respected the Indians and their customs and religion deeply enough that he was often suspected by his fellow pioneers of being some sort of turncoat.

He must have been extremely lonely, as all honest people are at times.

One of the saddest Boone tales has to do with the aftermath of his death, however, and of the grotesque and selfish actions of a few people who, in order to profit from his bones, had them (or someone's that were mistaken for his) dug up and transferred back to Kentucky, where there was to be a sort of monument to the achievements that, while he lived, were less vigorously honored.

What some folks won't do for a dollar!

Greywolf's gentle plea to all of us on this coffee house night, anyway, to respect the Native American burial grounds, put me in mind just now of this older story. We all want our cherished dead and their burial objects — rosaries, crucifixes, whatever — to rest undisturbed for as long as the grass shall grow, not a mere hundred years.

The Greywolf family and their Native peoples' message is one of respect for all living and dead, for human and animal creation and for earth itself.

It's a good message. I hope it lasts a thousand years or more.

American dreaming, singular and plural

This past weekend we celebrated the 217th anniversary of our nation's independence.

How many of our hearts and minds were caught up then in our own versions of the American dream?

We say "the" American Dream as if there were only one, but, more accurately from amidst so much diversity as now characterizes (and has always characterized) our country, we should perhaps speak of American dreams in the plural.

One man dreams of wealth and fame, power and prestige, the fortune to rise by his efforts above another.

One woman dreams of her whole people's welfare, their salvation from poverty and want, the self-respect of their young men who are tempted by despair and frustration and resentment.

Another man dreams of the economic freedom to create his own art, his own vision, his own monument to human aspiration and caring and hope.

Another woman dreams of singing, of standing on the stage at Carnegie Hall, or at the Grand Ole Opry.

Some people would say that Nashville, Tennessee, is the center of a lot of American dreaming, and that is where Anita's dream took her the other week, and to where she hopes it might return her in a not-so-distant future.

This first lingering in Nashville was quite exciting, really, its highlight undoubtedly being Anita's audition at the TNN studios for an at-this-point-hopeful appearance on the talent-search program *To Be a Star*.

The audition before producer Don Dashiel, who videotaped the performance to send to his boss in New York City, took place in a small trailer not far from the main TNN building.

Anita was at the top of her form for the two Stan LaGrange songs she presented, and the jolly producer seemed visibly taken by both singer and songs.

Later, she and I took in a matinee of the Grand Ole Opry, which was, itself, quite a lot of fun and gave Anita a glimpse of the stage on which she has always dreamed of standing.

The performers were alike and yet varied, giving us a glimpse of both the singularity and the plurality of this variety of American dreaming.

The most ethnic of the acts was a feisty Cajun country band from the heart of Louisiana, which reminded us that, though much of our vast musical heritage is marginalized, it persists in many forms, linguistic and otherwise.

The French-Creole of Louisiana stands beside the Texas blend of musics and languages of such as Freddy Fender and his Texas Tornados, who sing in both English and Spanish.

What is country music, after all? Where do country-western and Appalachian folk and bluegrass come together? Where do they move apart from each other?

What about the folk musics of other Hispanic, Asian, even Native American inhabitants of our soil? How does one folk's music become "country" while another folk's is left aside?

A problem with contemporary music, the industry of it with all its self-congratulation and its pomp and ceremony, is its corporate instinct to bulldoze its disparate elements into a common mold, thereby losing much of its diverse flavors.

There are counter-tendencies, though. Where two traditions truly meet, they change each other in unexpected ways. Even the dominant tradition is altered by its contact with a marginal one.

The influence of southwestern Mexican music on our own country-western heritage is undeniable, for example, and that and other influences are bound to grow as country music becomes more broad-based and its appeal more general.

Some people fear this sort of change, but much change is both necessary and good, especially when there's a mutual sharing of the best of distinct traditions.

A new country music (or musics) reflecting the variety of our faces, songs, and dreams, should, for this reason, be a welcome thing.

Already this American music comes from more directions than we often realize. The addition of Asian, or more Black and Hispanic and European, of Native American voices, faces, and song, is only natural and, I hope, inevitable.

Variety is the spice of all aspects of our lives, after all, music being no exception.

Holy cows! Another dream!

I thought I'd just awakened from another of my anxiety-ridden dreams about the approaching school season, when an apparition beside the bed confirmed that I was in for yet another cycle.

"Good ghosts, Braulio!" I exclaimed. "Anita's going to raise a fuss if she wakes up to the likes of you."

Just then Tasha appeared, too, but Anita kept on snoring, oblivious to the growing crowd in our bedroom.

"What are you doing here?" I asked my transmigrating friends. "How did you come?"

"Why do you dream?" Braulio asked eerily in return.

"How do dreams travel?" Tasha asked in cadaverous continuation of my nightmare.

At just that moment, I was caught up in a cloud of smoke. A growl, terrifying and deep, emerged from Braulio's throat. His eyes blazed red, his white hair stood on end, his face was pallid. A phantom hand reached out and grabbed my throat, dragging me back down toward the nightmarish depths of my abyss.

We stood there, just he and I, just Brett and Braulio, and he forced my gaze outward as if at myself.

A Jim Larson cow, *Far Side*ian, at the front of an unruly class, reciting poetry in English and Spanish against insouciant moo-ing.

"We are *vah-KEY-tuhs* of *new-ES-truhs O-bruhs*," the me-cow says, "cow-children of our deeds."

"Green how we love you green," the taunting cow-hoodlums respond, "puke green's how we love you best."

"But listen," the me-cow insists. "You are more than you think you are. Refer to the Buddha within you, the Christ within you, silly cows. *CO-mo say DEE-say en es-pan-YOL* (how do you say in Spanish) . . . 'All things are Buddha things . . . all things are Buddha things?'"

Just then Braulio laughed. His teeth shone like a Cheshire cat's, only framed in a ghoulish skull tucked under his arm like a headless horseman's. I screamed. His teeth were engulfed in a million gaping, cud-chewing cow teeth. Behind the teeth, at the nether-reaches of darkness, was the black hole into whose stinking bowels I was being sucked.

"All things are Buddha things," the me-cow kept repeating against the fear. "Consult the Christ-Buddha within you."

"The black moment," the me-cow remembered from his reading of mythologist Joseph Campbell, "is the moment when the real message of transformation is going to come. At the darkest moment comes the light."

Just then I saw Tasha. I was spinning in that darkness, (r)udderless, directionless, but there she was. Her voice was soothing now, life-giving, midwife, as it were, to countless rebirths of spiritual deaths and fears.

"What is it you're afraid of?" she gently asks.

"That I won't be good enough, that the children won't learn, that they'll moo me out of the classroom."

"But you're more than you think you are, Brett. There's no such thing as a merely ordinary mortal. Don't you know you're on the hero quest? As we all are. Only question is do we have what it takes. Will we crack or be cracked?"

Suddenly I knew that I was about to be compelled to answer that question for myself.

The demon cow-punk faces me, spewing spangled, mangled Spanglish over cud-drooling mandible.

"Totally awesome, dude . . . *macanoodle doodle* . . . gonna wrestle ya now like Jacob's awesome *'ombre.*"

Ay carumba, as Bart Simpson would say.

Locked with him now in mortal combat I think he has the upper hand, though for the first time this evening I am strangely calm.

He's pinned me, but I look him in the eye unconcernedly.

"This is my awesome classroom," I say, "and this is my dream, so get back to your place."

As he sits down at his desk — bright-eyed and swishy-tailed, and spitting his cud neatly into the spittoon — I notice that his face has metamorphosed into mine, then into Braulio's.

"The Buddha thing's inside you," Braulio whispers from the bottom of my bed, "but first you have to fight your inner demons."

"In any case," Tasha added from her perch beside the nightstand, "the mere fact of your nocturnal fretting speaks pretty well of your hero quest, clumsy as it may be. Now give it a rest and get some, yourself."

My ghosts disappeared and Anita rolled over in her sleep.

"Mmmmmm . . . is one of the kids up again, honey?"

On the art of making pictures with words

Sixty-one years ago, in the early days of our Great Depression, Laura Ingalls Wilder published the first volume in the now famous story of her even more remote childhood.

"Once upon a time, sixty years ago," she writes at the onset of the first book, "a little girl lived in the Big Woods of Wisconsin, in a little gray house made of logs."

Thus the journey begins.

Laura wrote and published her first eight "Little House" books between 1932 and 1943. The ninth book was published posthumously, in 1971, leaving off with the first four years of Laura's marriage to Almanzo Wilder, and with the beginning of their daughter Rose's childhood.

A few short Christmases ago, Anita and I sat down with our kids and started with the first book. In a few months we finished the ninth.

(If you've only seen the TV series, you owe it to yourself and your children to do the same. The books are infinitely superior to the show.)

I mention all of this, anyway, because of a recent discovery: a new book just published in 1993, called *Little House on Rocky Ridge*, which picks up with Laura, Almanzo, and Rose's trip from South Dakota's prairie to the Ozarks of Missouri.

"The journey continues," as the blurb on the back of the book announces.

The new book's author, Roger Lea MacBride, was a friend of the adult Rose and later became her lawyer, now the keeper of her papers and her estate. With this volume begins a new "Rocky Ridge" Little House series, with which he hopes to do the same for Rose's childhood as has already been done for Laura's.

At our house, we were excited to come on this story as it is being published for the first time, to be participants, as it were, in a bit of literary history in the making, a volume at a time.

At this writing halfway through July, we are already a hundred pages into it.

Rose loved to read, too, as her mother and grandmother did before her.

"Rose knew that words were a kind of magic that anybody could make," MacBride writes in one chapter. "Words told stories, which Rose loved better than anything. She thought about making up her own words, even her own language."

I remembered from the first "Little House" series, Laura's book *By the Shores of Silver Lake*, how Laura first becomes conscious of her gift for words as she becomes the eyes for her sister Mary, who has been blinded by scarlet fever.

That book contains some of the most beautiful passages I have ever read of a young writer's budding consciousness.

"Oh, Mary! The snow-white horse and the tall, brown man, with such a black head and a bright red shirt! The brown prairie all around — and they rode right into the sun as it was going down. They'll go on in the sun around the world."

Literalistic Mary reproves Laura for her impractical image, as she has done once before, but Laura is sensing what any good writer must learn.

"There were so many ways of seeing things and so many ways of saying them," she writes. Also: "Somehow that moment when the beautiful, free pony and the wild man rode into the sun would last forever."

Later, Laura tells Mary of "how the sun came up beyond Silver Lake, flooding the sky with wonderful colors while the flocks of wild geese flew dark against them, how thousands of wild ducks almost covered the water, and gulls flew screaming against the wind above it."

This time Mary is excited by the image.

"I heard them," she says. "Such a clamoring of wild birds, it was like a bedlam. And now I see it all. You make pictures when you talk, Laura."

This is a revelatory moment for the reader as well as for the young Laura because you see what it is to awaken to a gift, and you see foreshadowed the birth of these very stories that, over a hundred years later, you are now reading.

In this way, the image of a horse and a man and sun is eternal, contained within the many pictures that Laura's words have painted.

I have had a couple of students whose words come forth like that, as pictures.

This is a rare gift, perhaps, yet, as Rose thought as a child, its magic can happen to anyone, and has now and then in my classroom.

Everyone has at least one solid picture inside, waiting to be unleashed.

Martin Buber's unassuming philosophy of dialogue: "I encompass to whom I turn"

As I sit down at my desk to work, my first visitor is always the cat, who plops himself down in my workspace and reminds me of what's important.

I take a moment out and talk to him, pet him, stroke him.

As I interact with him, then, trying to approach him with my whole being, I think of the concept of dialogue developed by Martin Buber, whose philosophy is considered among the most positive and humane of this century.

"I am no philosopher, prophet, or theologian," he said at the end of his life, "but a man who has seen something and who goes to a window and points to what he has seen."

What he had seen before he died, some thirty years ago, is hard to explain except through examples. He does this particularly well in his little book *Meetings*, through a series of autobiographical meditations that reveal his experience and thought.

Early on, he speaks of his grandmother, whose communication with the people and the world about her was "so direct and so devoted."

He writes of his father, of how he would interact with a herd of horses, greeting them one at a time, "not merely in a friendly fashion but positively individually."

"This wholly unsentimental and wholly unromantic man," Buber writes, "was concerned about genuine human contact with nature, an active and responsible contact."

He also believed in person-to-person charity, not sightless philanthropy, or today's sort of bureaucratic welfarism.

"Even in his old age," Buber writes, his father "let himself be elected to the 'bread commission' of the Jewish community . . . and wandered tirelessly around the houses in order to discover the people's true wants and necessities; how else could that take place except through true contact!"

Through those experiences and others of his own — once, for example, while resting with his walking stick propped against a tree, he feels through that stick a kind of communion with the tree — Buber comes to an understanding of how we can relate to "the other."

"At that time," he writes, "dialogue appeared to me. For the speech of man is like that stick wherever it is genuine speech, and that means truly directed address . . . I encompass to whom I turn."

Instinctively, I sense that this is true. I try to live accordingly, engaging myself fully with whomever commands my attention at the moment, whether that be my cat, a family member, or a student.

I don't always succeed — Anita will tell you of my tendency to drift — but, by conscious effort, we sometimes arrive at such genuine moments of communion.

Buber himself, in this little treasure's closing fragment, writes of how, in his early years, he would have chosen books over people, but not so in his waning years.

"Not that I have had so much better experiences with men than with books; on the contrary, purely delightful books even now come my way more often than purely delightful men. But the many bad experiences with men have nourished the meadow of my life as the noblest book could not do, and the good experiences have made the earth into a garden for me."

He adds: "I knew nothing of books when I came forth from

the womb of my mother, and I shall die without books, with another human hand in my own."

It is this genuine human contact that matters, whether with person or with cat.

Take this cow tale to the bank!

The biggest news out at our place recently has been the arrival, via Louisville's airport, of Pablo López Ruf, an exchange student from La Plata, Buenos Aires, Argentina.

His arrival was almost eclipsed, though, by that of twenty-four of Larry and Marlene James's cows on the previous afternoon.

Nadina and Stephanie came shouting to Anita that there were cows across the street. She didn't believe them. Then she looked for herself.

"Oh. My. Gosh!" I heard her exclaim in slow motion, something like cousin Larry Appleton of television's *Perfect Strangers.*

She called my name and I looked myself. There they were, jogging over from James George's yard, out back of which they'd been grazing, loping across our front lawn toward the north side.

Disconcertedly, I went to the phone and relayed the news down the street.

Soon, Marlene was there, together with a visiting sister. Kyle rode up heroically on his four-wheeler, ready to round up those cows like some cowboy in a John Wayne movie.

It was his mom whose level-headedness saved the day, however, marshalling her son's exuberance to go get a bucket of grain, with which she lured them back where they'd come from.

She sent word through Nadina or Stephanie that she was sorry for the bother, but, in the end, I was sorry to see them go.

I've always had a thing for cows, you know, especially since the first time (as I've already alleged) that I heard one of them recite poetry in Spanish.

I must have been already pre-disposed toward them, though, by Aunt Gayle's and my grandpa Marion Kroessman's talk, years back, of purple cows they were always seeing around these parts.

None of these cows were purple, however, and, except for their noisy chomping and occasional moo, they were silent.

They were a well-mannered lot, neglecting to stomp on the dogwood tree in the west lawn or to uproot any of the little pines we have planted along the north.

Probably Kristy and Kyle's champion cows were among the twenty-four, which explains their generally good natures.

If you want to know why I really hated to see them go, it's because they'd hardly gotten started at eating the grass.

I guess Pablo will have to mow it now.

Buddy, can you spare some change?

I was in at the Leopold post office the other day, chatting with Ruth Bryant over a stack of correspondence and self-adhesive stamps, when the subject of change came up.

When the new stamps came out a while back, Ruth said, some folks were skeptical. There is a tendency, you know, to look at all and any change through severely jaundiced eyes.

Sometimes, though, a healthy dose of it is exactly what the doctor ordered. Such has been the case with the self-stick stamps. Those same folks who once looked at them askance, now ask for them by name. At last, a stamp with no aftertaste.

Would that all really significant social, political, moral, educational change were so clear and easy to embrace as the non-stick postage stamp.

Fact is that it's almost inevitably painful, and never entirely clear.

I have just finished reading, in Spanish, a novel about religious and social change in late 19th-century Spain. The author is Benito Pérez Galdós, the Spanish Dickens, best Spanish realist since Cervantes three hundred years earlier.

In this novel, Spanish Catholic traditionalism, in the form of matriarch Doña Perfecta, meets new ideas of religious and social liberalism, in the person of Pepe Rey, the city-educated nephew who wants to marry her daughter.

Sadly, as happens in so many other places and times in history, the two perspectives do not truly meet, and the novel's fragile hope is met instead (at least for the moment) by tragedy.

In our country, thanks to the unsuperstitious faith of such as Jefferson and Washington, our national faith is independent of our state, and tolerates a remarkable degree of pluralism, though there remain tensions: creationist vs. evolutionist; school prayer vs. strict separationist; fundamentalist vs. reformist.

This sort of tension exists among all of our American groups, and is not necessarily harmful, if we can keep from violent reactions and counteractions that sometimes doom any effort at mutual conciliation.

The recent and historical accord in the Middle East is illustrative.

Will extremists among Israeli and Palestinian patriots allow themselves to move beyond Holocaust-era defensive politics, into a gray but promising era of negotiation and dialogue?

Such change is never easy, but God knows it is necessary if we are to learn to keep from hating — and killing — each other.

Religious fundamentalism gets in the way by negatively assuming that such conflicts are irrevocable, predestined, apocalyptic.

Expansive religious faith, on the other hand, defined by Catholic insistence on human free will, allows for the option of mutual tolerance, of transformed perceptions, of new understanding.

The Christian doctrine of charity — "love your enemy as yourself" — is at the heart of all spiritual teaching, though it is distorted when we insist on its application only within our chosen group, when we only trust to mistrust the other group.

One example of this "trust to mistrust" mentality—this happened in the small south-central Indiana town where I went to high school — is when a predominantly white community blackballs the only physician in town, because he is ethnically a Filipino.

It also happens here when, in the narrow, established interests of extended family and community, we shut out the business of someone who comes to us from another county, as has happened in recent history.

It doesn't always happen this way, but sometimes it does, and then we all lose out in ways that we may not have imagined.

In the realm of education, wherever we go, the most common conflict is between those who suggest new methods to meet a changed student body and world, and those who insist on the traditional virtues of our American frontier's one-room schoolhouse.

In any future discussion of education in the real-life context of Perry County, the best of both arguments will have to be brought to bear.

All change is not necessarily good, but its absence is almost inevitably bad.

America is founded on it, after all, and will only thrive on an inspired continuation of real, even radical transformation.

Salvador Dalí and the persistence of imagination

If you should chance to visit my classroom out at Perry Central, be sure to take in the Salvador Dalí art print on the east wall.

It's new this fall, and it's been the source of a lot of conversation.

The scene is a bleak, barren landscape, littered by such everyday objects as elongated clocks drooping from the jutting branch of a rotted tree trunk, or from some mysteriously placed table.

Then there's a weird creature (dog? camel? what?) with a hairy protuberance that, if not for my classes' further anatomical investigations (which suggest an eyelash), might pass as a mustache.

The creature is either dead or dying, lying there on its side, exhausted and apparently panting.

The title (in French here) is something like "Persistence of Memory." The artist (recently dead) is not French but Spanish. He's this century's undisputed master of Spanish surrealism, a school of art that represents human experience through fantastic, dreamlike imagery.

This art is not like the abstract splotches of color of a Jackson Pollock canvas, devoid of traditionally evident form. The forms are visible, but distorted. The art is not purely abstract, but it is distinctly modern. Interpretation is not an easy matter.

Gale Garner and Jackie Wright, for instance, encountering it in unison on a warm August afternoon, experienced considerable difficulty in that respect.

Gale responded skeptically to my tentative attempt at explaining the composition: "Oh," he finally ventured. "I thought maybe the clocks were just melting in the heat."

To which Jack added some characteristically pointed remark about the artist's heat-induced insanity.

I have to admit that Dalí was, in life, a bit eccentric. Also, the windowless classroom (cooled to a brisk 85° rather than 95° Fahrenheit) felt hot enough to melt anything, captive scholars and professor included.

Dalí, however, is not to be trifled with. There is method to his madness.

Among those who sense that is my former student Denise Richard, who stopped in one day after school.

"I love it," she said. "It's one of my favorite paintings."

Barbara Spear loved it for her son, who she was sure would kill for it. I'm happy to report that he didn't have to, since Barb promptly ordered it and another Dalí print for him.

Then there's David Hubert, who, having previously explored the artist's work in one of Lynn Dauby's art classes, suggested to our literature class that the melting clocks might represent how memory works in us over time, each detail melting into each other, persisting through various distortions and fantasies.

Whatever the case, I'm glad I put the print up there, and that it has provoked so much comment, even if much of that comment is bewildered.

It's a source of some befuddlement to me, after all, that so many people seem so piteously bereft of imagination.

For their book reviews, for instance, one student reads Kafka's *Metamorphosis*, another Orwell's *Animal Farm*, and all either one can see is that men don't really turn into cockroaches nor animals take over farms.

Have these poor mortals never had a really vivid nightmare,

or exercised imagination? Have we immunized our children, ourselves, against dreams?

Those are a couple of the questions that most deeply puzzle me, in the end, while imaginatively I have no problem believing in humans who metamorphose into insects, or in an animal-run totalitarian farm.

If men can act like animals, after all, why not turn into them, or they into men?

God bless Salvador Dalí, anyway, for his maniacally sane perspective. May he be kept through the persistence of our imaginations, crazed as to ordinary folks they may appear.

Drive-by shoutings and other devilry

Definitely, I am blessed to make my home in Perry County, Indiana rather than in Harris County, Texas where I lived briefly before coming home.

Houston may boast a more varied cultural life than we enjoy here, but all of that comes with a price.

Let me illustrate. Living there, I might be drive-by *shot* at; out here in the proverbial "middle of nowhere," more likely drive-by *shouted* at.

When boys can't be men, they'll be boys, and in that case a good cussing is certainly preferable to a bullet to the head.

The joke, I know, is in poor taste. I acknowledge that with full apologies and in the spirit of self-effacement. It's just that this is the sort of pitiful bromide that is liable to shoot through a weary teacher's brain as the night-blackened car cruises past, brave obscenities trailing after it.

It occurred to me, of course, that they were merely calling me what they wouldn't dare call me in the classroom. So I'm crushed! I went on, dripping with righteous sarcasm. I wouldn't have given the oaths a second thought if it hadn't been for the broken basketball rim. And the damaged porch light that doesn't work now, either.

That was Friday the 17th. Of September, not October. The work was done before the family and I made it home from the Perry Central football game.

The yard swing was easily enough removed from the roof, and its upended frame from the driveway.

The picnic table, slightly damaged but repairable, was found a few hours later where it had been tossed over the hill behind the house, in the overgrowth approaching Indiana 37.

All of this equipment (along with our car), during a month and a half of the year's finest weather, was necessarily locked up in the garage. Toilet paper was pulled off the trees. Water off a teacher's back, if it weren't for the destruction, which didn't amuse.

On another night, before our Argentine exchange student moved into a different family's house, he did help me catch one tic-tacker.

There were others, but we just cornered one. He took down what toilet paper was left, urging me all the while not to tell Coach Wagner on him.

He'd heard about those vandals, he said, and was sorry about that. They'd given good boys and girls like him a bad name.

"We just want to throw a little toilet paper in some trees," he explained, "and enjoy the thrill of being chased. Till we're all growed up and can't do that no more."

I understood the sentiment (having, my first year, enjoyed the thrill of playful chase) and didn't tell Coach Wagner on him. But I allowed to myself that they could still all do with a little heat. And a good deal of sober reflection.

In some ways, they're like the rascal Coyote in Greywolf's traditional stories, always sticking their noses into places where they don't belong.

Example: Peering in windows and studying your every private move before the deed.

Example: Ringing the doorbell late at night, waking wife and children, compelling you to come outside and play.

Example: Returning again and again, without thought that maybe you've got more pressing duties than picking up after them — planning a lesson, for instance, or grading papers, or tending a sick child in the hospital.

Then there's the fact that they start on Sept. 17, for heaven's sake, when really that activity should, at the very most, be limited to Halloween week.

Ultimately, of course, it comes back to the abusiveness, the latest instance of which, at our place, was the smearing of manure on a glass door.

I like to humor children whenever I can, but I've concluded that to continue looking the other way while good kids throw toilet paper is to tacitly enable the bad actors to destroy property and smear excrement on doors and windows.

Not all county adults share my perspective, of course. I know of one lady who not only knows the names of everyone involved in the initial vandalism of my property, but has openly laughed about it to a friend of ours.

Shame on her, and on all the boys and girls in this county who refuse to be men and women — as all of us, right here as well as in Harris County, could certainly do worse than aspiring after.

A modest proposal for neutralizing vandals

Lest anyone misunderstand, let me assure the gentle reader that the proposal that follows is made in jest, in the spirit of satire.

I used humor as a means of lightening the mood after the previous essay ("Drive-by shoutings . . .") and of even poking a little fun at myself. After all, as a teacher and as one who has been called, once or twice, a "bleeding heart liberal," I can only have meant more or less the exact opposite of what I seem to argue at this essay's end in defense of my sham proposal.

My recent frustrations on account of the clandestine activities of area teens, made public in some detail in a previous column, left me to ponder the probability or improbability of devising a solution.

I was about to give it up as a lost cause when my oldest daughter discovered, within the grill on our back deck, the rotting carcass of a possum that (God knows when) some of those miscreants had picked up off the road for my next barbecue.

The stench of decomposing flesh reminded me of the 18th-century British satirist Jonathan Swift, author of *Gulliver's Travels*, whose fairly immodest proposal in another instance resolved the public dilemma of what to do about starving children in Ireland where he had grown up and been educated.

I understand that some folks in Swift's day got a little squeamish about his idea of selling well-fattened human infants to garnish the tables of the rich, but the fellow did have a marketable scheme.

With modern advances in advertising theory and technique, it might have flown — just as today in rural Indiana we market T-shirts and cooking ideas for road kill.

What I propose, more or less, is that, with one stone, we neutralize a couple of pesky birds:

Teachers and parents in Perry County face the problem of what to do with their young vandals.

The president faces the problem of foreign policy hotspots like Somalia and Bosnia.

My plan quite efficiently answers both concerns: by using state and local law enforcement to conscript Halloweeners, appealing to the National Guard only as a last resort, we can get those hapless idlers out of our hair and at the same time contribute to the international peace.

Bored teens would benefit from the mere fact of having something to do, and I wouldn't doubt that, after a reasonable period of service, a few of them might even come back alive — and better for the wear.

Teachers and parents would have their yards back (though in the resulting unemployment some teachers might have trouble holding onto them).

Soldiers would benefit by being spared for when they're clearly needed, such as when another sheikh with the raw materials for a nuclear arsenal messes again with our sacred supply of oil.

The whole nation would benefit from our president's being able to concentrate on domestic issues, with which he is professedly most at ease.

An obvious flaw in my plan, of course, is that there are only some 19,000 of us in the county, and considerably fewer teens: demand would quickly outstrip supply.

That's no problem at all, though, if we make of this a national juvenile corrections plan for all teen offenders: the mother of all boot camps.

Some bleeding-heart liberal may have other ideas.

My friends Braulio and Tasha, for example, with whom I first shared this proposal, suggested a variety of what I must say are, for the local palate, far too immodest alternatives.

One is that, rather than send teens off to Bosnia, we devise something for them to do at home.

In cases of discipline, involve them in a required community service, but such as would require their interaction with responsible adults and with other teens who are not necessarily in trouble, in a pride-building activity similar to the floodwall mural project.

Another suggestion is to open a club where teens could gather all year long to mingle, dance, play video games — all without the temptation of alcohol.

I told my friends to get real.

We can spare the teaching jobs. Teachers are paid too much for nine months' work, anyway, and might find that being unemployed inspires them to become professional golfers or something — productive citizens worthy of large salaries.

Just send the rascals to Bosnia, for heaven's sake. There's a solution that's uncomplicated and easy to implement.

On peace, thanksgiving, and apple seeds

I was taken a bit off guard the other day when David Hubert declared that he knew why I didn't own a gun.

"Because you're a pacifist," he announced jovially, stepping aside then for the usual barrage of commentary from other students, intent on knowing how I'd protect myself in the event of an intrusion.

When David said it, I wasn't sure how to respond.

I felt like Cuban philosopher Jorge Valls, who spent years as a prisoner of conscience under both rightist dictator Batista and leftist dictator Castro.

"I don't know if I am violent or nonviolent," he says, "but I don't believe in violence as a way to obtain justice."

All quibbling aside, though, I was pleased by that new assessment of my character, and I accept it. There are warriors enough in our world; it won't be harmed by the addition of one more genuine pacifist.

I am always surprised at the violent reaction that word elicits from some people, as if a peaceable disposition were distinctly un-American.

First of all, I don't believe it is.

Quakerism didn't originate in America, for instance, but it came here for religious freedom, to escape persecution in England for, among other things, the refusal of its adherents to bear arms.

Name me a more American city than William Penn's "City of Brotherly Love," home of the Liberty Bell.

It is true that the Quaker colony also became a focal point of revolutionary fighting against Great Britain, but members of the Society of Friends have been able to maintain that basic pacifism without their Americanism being seriously questioned.

The anti-war fervor of our Sixties and Seventies may indeed have brought abuses by some who aligned themselves with pacifist goals, yet resorted to violence against returning Vietnam soldiers.

Activists today, to the extent that they bring deliberate physical harm to their philosophical adversaries, are also impostors if they claim pacifist goals, for the ends do not justify the means.

If we look deeply into our complex histories, though, beneath the glossy surfaces that are most often projected, we see deep in our American heritage a populist instinct against violence, even as our advances across the continent were driven by violence.

If imperfectly realized in our histories, the instinct toward a more peaceable kingdom is perfectly embodied in the sweet tall tale of Johnny Appleseed, who traversed wilderness and frontier with neither gun nor arrows nor thought of how he'd protect himself in the event of an intrusion.

Of the frontier heroes of my imaginative boyhood, Johnny Appleseed has always been among the first.

I like that he wouldn't hunt, that he was honored by pioneer and Indian alike, that he befriended animals and children.

I don't care what part of the story that has grown up around this historical figure is fact or fiction.

I agree with Robert Price, who, writing in 1954 (quoted today in an author's note to a children's picture book), suggested that "when a folk tale attains the status of a myth and embodies a cherished ideal of the people, then its true worth no longer lies merely in the dead facts that may have inspired it, but in the new, living, and creating force that it has become in the present."

In my own life, my peaceable instinct has of course been imperfectly realized, as I gave in to the urge to spank rather than instruct a child, or entertained the perilous thought of throttling a bothersome student. If the peaceable side of my nature is what has been rising to the top, however, I have ample reason for thanksgiving.

May it continue to do so.

I should rather be linked with the world's peacemakers than with its avengers, after all.

May I always sing the peace songs of our enigmatic and unpeaceful Sixties.

1994: Talk of the County

Complex truths about human relationships

Some of you know that for a while last fall we had an exchange student in our home, and that, among my two brothers, is one ten years my junior who's engaged to be married later this year.

The two facts are linked to each other by the recent visit of Pablo with his mother and sisters, and of Kirk with his pretty fiancée.

Pablo's mother, María Rosa, is refined and beautiful. His sisters — María and Sofía, the older ones, and Elena, the baby — seem fashioned into that same image.

Elena would not talk much, but otherwise made herself at home. She played with our girls and hauled around the cat, who seemed bemused but nonchalant about all of her unsolicited attentions.

Sofía and María speak English like their brother and have taught some to Elena, who, in kindergarten, is also being introduced to some phrases.

María speaks and comprehends especially well, and was more than capable of getting her mom around New York City before the flight to Indiana.

I am impressed. I wish our schoolchildren started their foreign language studies in elementary school. Then perhaps more than an elite minority would come out of high school with the beginnings of a competency.

In Argentina, of course, there's also a difference between foreign language study in most public schools versus some private schools.

If I were to propose the addition at Perry Central of serious foreign language study from grades K-8, I would simply be told that there isn't the money.

The same is true in Buenos Aires. As societies, we often have our priorities amiss. We'll pay more to be entertained, as a friend of mine is fond of saying, than to be educated.

A lot is being attempted these days in foreign language education, and I look forward to new directions that may be on my horizon, but I can't help supposing that we set a lot of kids up for failure because we wait too long to put them on the road to certain kinds of learning.

In any case, it was very nice to meet the women in Pablo's family. I was charmed.

The visit was also healing, in a sense — healing of a separation that occurred in October, and of the idle words of people who don't even know us, who've been whispering that Pablo must have left our home because we'd mistreated him.

The truth of all human relations is inevitably more complicated than that, riddled with misunderstandings and gratitudes, never in any simple way.

I should leave this to my philosopher brother, though, who from his Classical studies could explain to us what Plato would have said on the subject.

Kirk and I do often talk philosophy to each other, whether ancient or modern, sacred or profane.

I've become closest to him within the last couple of years, when our experiences in many respects, unique as they remain, have seemed to converge.

I know he worries our mom with his changing notions.

My feeling, though, is that she shouldn't worry so much, because Kirk's on an inward road that he has to travel in order to find enduring peace.

If we wrestle alone with our unique lonelinesses, that's no more nor less than what we all have to do if we're ever to encounter the strength of wisdom within us.

We can only encounter that healing by turning inward in full honesty, without fear of what is yet unknown.

At the same time, though, we need to have someone there to share that road with us.

I'm happy that Kirk's found Rebecca, and she him.

They make a pretty couple, and I think an intelligent one, joyously promising.

I remain childishly pleased with both of these visits.

The Blizzard-of-94 snowed-in story

IN WHICH A CERTAIN COUNTY ESSAYIST REMINISCES ABOUT A FEW STORIES EITHER SNOW-BOUND OR NOT, AND A MENAGERIE OF OTHER STUFF THAT HE HOPES WILL PLEASE THE READER

Now, this story begins thanks to some others by an Albert Bigelow Paine, author of *The Hollow Tree Snowed-In Book*, published in 1910 by Harper and Brothers, illustrated by one J. M. Conde.

A copy of this book was given to my grandpa on his eighth birthday: "Happy birthday to Marion from Aunt Claudine, Nov. 29, 1919."

The book's cover is green with white lettering and snowfall, black flourishes and bordering for contrast, and an orange sunset. The treehouse is green. Mr. Crow, the host, looks out from a window. Mr. Rabbit and Mr. Turtle approach along a snow-laden branch.

The book's binding is weak, but the stories still delight.

We can relate to the animals as they get set for the approaching snowstorm, wishing no harm but knowing that they can't change the blizzard from its course.

Personally, I've always found a deep snow to be the prettiest of winter landscapes, perfect antidote to the gray drabness that otherwise pervades our winters.

This is especially so if we can stay cozily at home, untouched by such troubles as the power outages that, for others' sake, we hope are soon relieved, in the meantime hoping that those folks all find other shelter.

Otherwise, as Mr. Crow said during the storyteller's long-ago winter, "it might snow as much as it liked as long as we had plenty of wood and things to eat inside," and our tempers were not too short.

It turns out that the animals were set, with warmth and food and stories for the blizzard's long assault.

All of them "lit their pipes, and looked into the fire, and thought a little before talking — thinking, of course, of what a good time they were having, and how comfortable and nice it was to be inside and warm when such a big snow was falling outside."

Soon, in response to Mr. Robin's pleasant saying about the wood-gatherers being the strongest bunch of animals "outside of a menagerie," we are regaled by the animals' entertaining versions of what that word "menagerie" might mean.

Everyone has a pleasant notion, but only Mr. Dog has ever seen one from the inside, and can supply the first-hand (if naive) account of what one is, and a warning to the other animals to never join one.

Mr. Dog's story, then, of how he followed Mr. Man to that old-fashioned circus, is the first snowed-in story, followed quickly by Mr. Coon's account of how he almost became a part of just such a menagerie.

This book, though I don't recall hearing its stories as a child, has become a favorite.

The humor is as sharp and sophisticated, in a way, as Mark Twain's.

That has something to do with Mr. Paine's judicious use of voice, of dialect, which not everyone can do with such happy effect.

He succeeds with turn-of-the-century American speech as well as A. A. Milne succeeds with British speech in *The World of*

Pooh, a genuinely hilarious book that must nevertheless fall rather flat without some awareness of the word-play that drives much of its humor.

Howard R. Garis's Uncle Wiggily books succeed less perfectly to my adult ear, the language itself often descending to an inane sort of childishness, and the moralisms to a too-facile sugar-coated sweetness.

A part of me remains fond, nevertheless, of the kindly rabbit gentleman and his feminine sidekick Nurse Jane Fuzzy Wuzzy, mostly due to the memory of hearing those stories on my grandma's voice.

"So if the wheelbarrow doesn't catch cold when it runs after the train of cars to get a ride around the block," one story nonsensically ends, Grandma and Mr. Garis will next tell me and Todd about Uncle Wiggily's adventure with a camel.

My brother and I would laugh childishly at the preposterous "if" clause, hardly able to wait for another night's story.

What I most remember on Grandma's voice, though, and what stands the test of time better than that, is the Hoosier poetry of James Whitcomb Riley, which I will always recite with Grandma's accent.

Most remembered and recited are the famous ones: "Little Orphant Annie," "The Raggedy Man," "Our Hired Girl."

There are others, though, such as one about a "circus-day parade" that Mr. Paine's Hollow-Tree animals would certainly have appreciated.

They would have wondered about the gleeful descriptions of that frightening menagerie of "tame" animals, the "shambling camels," for instance, "masticating as they came."

No telling what delights we would experience in their contemplation of the mysteries of that new word: "masticating."

As these animals of the Big Deep Woods of Dream sit down with their pipes, commencing this other story, I also catch the image of an old picture of my dad, wearing blue jeans and flannel shirt, a pipe in his mouth.

Though he no longer smokes, the smell of that pipe remains genuinely sweet to me, rich and evocative.

So do the best of all remembered poems and stories.

Essayists tend to personalize their columns

I enjoyed reading Rural News the other day, particularly the various correspondents' personalized responses to January's big snow.

That "personalizing," though Ruth Loesch felt obliged to shorten hers, was what I most enjoyed. It tends to produce some interesting writing.

Even so, I understand Ruth's reluctance to be criticized for dwelling too long in print on her own life. I've been chastened, too, by a recent Hot Line caller who reminds me that this column is called "Talk of the County."

The caller asked why I've named the column as I have while seeming to produce something very different.

Every good question deserves a thoughtful answer.

This one begins with a little background.

When the folks at the office asked me to name my new column, I thought of E. B. White's former essays for *The New Yorker* magazine.

You may know E. B. White as author of children's classics like *Charlotte's Web*, but he also wrote for adults.

I love his "Talk of the Town" essays, some of which appeared in a book called *One Man's Meat*, and which, on the whole, had very little to do with New York City.

He had gone to live on a farm in Maine, and he wrote about that place as any good writer must, simply as he met it. He didn't write about his neighbors by name, but they were present. One column was devoted entirely to the review of a book he'd read on that farm but that had more to do with fascism in Europe, which enraged him.

When I named my column Talk of the County, then, I wanted that phrase to be read broadly.

Perry County does not exist in a vacuum. It's connected to other places and people, which inevitably reflect back on us.

Writing *of* is not the same as writing *about*.

When a student asks what a story is about — take *Charlotte's Web*, for example — one is tempted to say about a farm girl, her pig, Wilbur, and his spider, Charlotte.

That would be false, though, on anything but a superficial level.

The story is really about some big human experiences like love, devotion, friendship, death, growing up. Spider and pig are mere symbols of ourselves.

Similarly, when I write an essay touching on family and visits, the essay is never really about me or my family.

The real meaning lies beneath the surface and is necessarily expressed by reference to how I've encountered it.

I am writing about an experience that may be shared personally by all of us, some small part of which I attempt to elaborate on or explain.

That's why I hesitate to entirely banish my family from this column.

I'll try to sharpen the county focus. The essayist's voice, though, has to remain personal.

As I continue writing these essays, anyway, in whatever guise or shape, I'm glad that folks keep talking about them.

From my perspective, that's the best news, and another thing I'd originally intended by talk *of* the county.

A chat with a local mouse

This one's for Stephanie and Moonstar, two people I know who've experienced what it is to love a mouse.

I once read a story of a man who loved pigs and wouldn't butcher his. His neighbors thought him an oddity, I think, but it was a beautiful story. I'll have to track it down again.[8]

To love a pig, after all, or to love a mouse, is surely not such a strange thing. It could happen to anyone.

I was thinking of that the other night, anyway, my mind turning sentimentally from more melancholy thoughts, when I noticed a mousy creature who was peacefully observing me.

He interrupted my thoughts with this observation.

"It's really not, you know. So strange, I mean. But grown-ups tend to forget. They think animals are just something to eat, or to keep out of the cupboards."

"Pleased to meet you," I said, clearing my throat and trying not to sound too surprised.

"Pleasure's mine," he answered. "Just call me Michael B — B, for short. The B is for Ben."

"Okay, B," I mumbled, unable to keep from wondering to what I owed this preternatural visit.

Everyone knows, after all, that neither mice nor pigs (not even my ubiquitous cows) can really talk.

"Who says we can't?" (B had again read my mind.)

"I'm sorry," I said. "I just thought—"

"Anyway," he said, "you just shouldn't have forgotten. You should have remembered."

"Remembered?"

"Remember Frederick?" he said, and then I did.

"Frederick. Isn't he that Spanish bull that Munro Leaf wrote about, who disappointed the bullfight recruiters by just sitting quietly in the middle of the ring and smelling all the flowers in the lovely ladies' hair?"

"I hesitate to call you dummy," B answered politely, "but you're really much worse off than I'd thought."

"That's not him?" I cried.

"No! That's Ferdinand. He's a friend of the family, too, but not as closely related."

That's right, I thought, beginning to recall, as B was now recounting it, that charming Leo Leonni story.

Frederick, you see, belonged to a chatty family of field mice, who were gathering supplies for the winter.

All except Frederick, who appeared to be loafing (for which his family reproved him), but who was actually gathering sun rays, and colors, and words against the cold dark winter days.

When they were running out of those other supplies, they called on Frederick, who delivered warm thoughts and poetry to tide them over.

"But Frederick," they all said when he was finished, "you're a poet."

Frederick blushed, took a bow, and said shyly, "I know it."

I felt ashamed for having forgotten that mouse's humanity.

"I'm sorry," I said. "I guess I should remove the poison?"

"You might have at least made an offering," he said. "Spread some noodles outside of the bag, under the house."

Mice people have to eat too, I agreed.

"I know your little girl's mouse friends," B said, "and you can tell her not to worry about Whiskers, because he's not lost — he's staying with us. I knew I could chat with you, too, when I heard you talking to her the other day, soothing her sad mood and tender feelings about the animal creation. Moonstar always said you were okay, but I hadn't been sure.

"Oh, by the way," he said at last, just as I could see he was set to scurry away, perhaps sensing the approach of my cat, the one Whiskers had apparently given the slip, "if you should ever get too weary of what you're doing now, think of following your old dream and becoming a forester. A naturalist, like Moonstar. We animals can always use another human who remembers that we're all related."

---

8   A narrative poem, actually, by John Sterling Harris, called "The Assassination of Emma Gray"; from Cracroft and Lambert's anthology of Latter-day Saint literature *A Believing People*.

Mexican ritual leads to grace and healing

Last fall, while watching after a sick child in the hospital, I took the occasion to re-read a book called *Refuge*, by Terry Tempest Williams.

It's a book too rich in its experience to be trusted to a single reading, or to be adequately summarized here.

Published in 1991 by Pantheon Books in New York City, the story occurs in the very different setting — amidst our Rocky Mountains — of the Great Salt Lake valley, home to her Mormon forebears.

Terry writes of the experience of change, that inevitable part of mortality.

As a daughter, she faces change in the fact of her mother's dying of cancer.

As a naturalist and environmental activist, she faces it in the loss of habitat for the birds she follows, their freshwater refuge altered by the rising levels of Great Salt Lake.

These separate threads of story are intertwined in a beautiful narrative that's ever conscious of the natural relationships that have always existed, and of the disruptions that occur when we are careless of these environments.

Change is inevitable, as is the sorrow inherent in any loss, but there is also a healing grace that helps us cope.

These are universal truths.

Had Williams grown up along the Ohio River instead of by Great Salt Lake, the essence of her story might not have been significantly different.

In contemplation of her own reluctance to give up her mother, and of her mother's desire to just live "in the heart of each day," she remembers Buddha's teaching that there are two kinds of suffering: one leading to more suffering, the other leading to suffering's end.

She tells us, in that context, of one day encountering a barn swallow caught up in a barbed-wire fence.

When she frees it, the bird's heart is racing: it has exhausted itself in struggle.

She places it among some blades of grass and watches it relax, breathing more shallowly, until its chest becomes still in death.

"Dying doesn't cause suffering," she then observes. "Resistance to dying does."

This is true not just of the one who dies, but of those who mourn.

It's natural that we do mourn.

We all need rituals to help us let go, whether the child to release a beloved grandparent, or the grandparent to release a little child.

Williams is right, then, in the instinct that drives her toward Mexico after her mother's passing, to experience there a traditional village's Day of the Dead, a sort of combination of All Hallows Eve and a de-militarized Memorial Day.

Sometimes, the individual requires something else, something uniquely hers.

So it is that she went to Mexico, in search of a personal ritual to finish the healing that, within her own spiritual heritage, had already been commenced.

At one point, in that traditional village, "filled with gratitude for the graciousness of these people," she walks with the procession toward a cemetery.

They spread a pathway of marigold petals for the dead to follow.

Later, a woman shows Terry her own family's graves, then motions to the beautiful sky with "clouds like roses," indicating that the dead are still among us.

She gives Terry a marigold, her mother's springtime flower, and Terry takes it home where, with her husband, in the middle of Great Salt Lake, she scatters the petals in a gesture of her own healing.

The refuge that she finds from sorrow is within her, as it necessarily is for each of us.

May this be so of all who have suffered any loss in this season, or who will suffer losses in any other.

Writer's block ends at the bullfights

My dad will perhaps forgive me this little piece about the time he was sick at a bullfight.

That was some thirty years ago when we lived in Torrance, California. It happened across the border in Tijuana, where we had planned a day's excursion.

The reason it comes to mind just now is that I have writer's block.

The only way past writer's block is to write, which reminds me of what *Houston Chronicle* essayist Leon Hale once wrote about some advice he'd received from his first editor.

There's no excuse, short of one's own death, the editor had said, for missing a column. If you're sick, write about being sick.

So Leon took him at his word, writing years later for another editor (while holed up sick in some obscure Texas motel room) of a more colorful time when he'd been sick in Mexico.

That's how I come to the inglorious theme of my dad sick at the bullfight in Tijuana.

That, and the contemplation of the bullfighting art in my Spanish classroom, which consists of a dark velvet painting that fellow teacher Gary Cooper unloaded on me, and a laminated poster announcing a bullfight in Spain.

The black velvet is forgettable, but it goes well with the other black velvet inherited from the basement of Kurt and Paula Cooper's old rental house, a Moorish-looking woman with green fan and veil, who, to my romantic imagination, embodies the south of Spain.

The poster is, on the other hand, quite imposing.

In bold, black print, in the popular Spanish idiom, it announces a GRANDIOSE BULLFIGHT for 5:30 Sunday evening.

There, if a superior will gives permission and the weather doesn't get in the way, six MAGNIFICENT AND BRAVE BULLS will be pierced, bludgeoned, and killed by the spear.

The names of the men who'll wave the red capes, to the cheers of the pretty ladies in the crowd, are prominently mentioned.

The picture is dramatic: the picador dressed elegantly amidst flashes of blue, gold, and pink; the wave of the red cape; the charging bull with colorful spears already lodged between his shoulders.

I would like to portray for you that the brutal spectacle of this savage sport was what sickened my dad, but that would not be true.

We never even got to see the fight, because Dad was already sick as we entered the stadium.

We turned right around — my little brother Todd and I, both my parents, and Dad's mom, Evelyn Sanders, who was then visiting — and Mom took over at the wheel, driving the distance to our house.

I think that she, who cried at the death of Bambi's mom, was secretly pleased, as in retrospect I probably am, too.

Though not a vegetarian, I have inherited my mom's sensitivities against the senseless slaughter of God's other living creatures.

I suppose it was the old European heritage, embodied in this Spanish drama of man against nature and in Melville's *Moby Dick*, that brought the mighty buffalo to near extinction.

The old Greek story is of how Theseus went into the labyrinth, a terrible and deadly maze at whose center rested the

Minotaur, and heroically killed that half-man, half-bull eater of human flesh.

The Spanish custom of bullfighting is a deliberate restaging of that ancient myth.

The heroic Spaniard fairly spits in death's eye.

This is a tradition losing appeal to a younger generation in Spain and throughout Latin America, who prefer the somewhat less savage spectacle of soccer.

For a truly harrowing account of a traveler caught up in a crowd of soccer fans in a Costa Rican city, read Paul Theroux's entertaining book *The Old Patagonian Express*.

Take comfort, meanwhile, in my own escape from the savagery of that bullfight in Tijuana.

My innocence was preserved for another day. And Dad did mend.

Meditations on Miranda's baptism

If you follow the TV program *Northern Exposure*, you probably saw Shelly and Holling's baby, Miranda, receive her Catholic baptism the other night.

Shelly is an innocently believing Catholic who worries about Holling's rugged (though not unspiritual) agnosticism and who tries to keep him from too much interaction with the itinerant priest who's come to do the job.

Holling ends up getting in some intense theological debates with the fervent priest, in the context of friendly drinking and arm-wrestling and such.

When innocent Shelly confesses before her daughter's baptism, she confides in the priest her disappointment in his behavior.

A man of the cloth should be someone above the common rung of humanity, she thinks.

The priest tells her that, when it's time for the baptism, she'll feel better.

The miracle is how God uses each of us within our humanity to accomplish holy purposes.

She is skeptical, but, when the time comes, the priest proves right.

He speaks of the African proverb that a village raises a child, and speaks to the community that will participate in the raising up of this child.

He speaks of how, in our humanity, God sees us and forgives the truly repentant of their sins.

The child's head is sprinkled, and at that moment Maggie flies overhead in the plane she has just triumphantly built.

Spirits soar with it; troubled hearts heal. Shelly, in her innocent faith, is comforted.

I am moved, too, as in many other episodes of this profoundly intimate show.

Such as when Joel's beloved uncle dies, and the whole community of his exile labors lovingly to find ten Jews to stand with him and perform the sacred Kaddish, the traditional prayer for the dead.

The Jews are recruited for money, but in the end Joel senses that he doesn't need them.

The episode ends with Joel reciting Kaddish before his own non-Jewish community — explaining the prayer's significance to its members and reciting, then, in Hebrew.

He is clothed with the traditional prayer shawl and cap.

Before praying, he has briefly explained to those assembled why he's called them instead of the others: because he's learned that this community is his family, and that the prayer circle should consist of a society of friends, not of paid mercenaries.

Those people's sharing in that moment is something holy, affecting me as deeply as a revelation.

Now, in the spiritual tradition that I adopted some years ago, we do not hold with infant baptisms.

"And their little children need no repentance, neither baptism," the Book of Mormon scripture reads. "Behold, baptism is unto repentance to the fulfilling the commandments unto the remission of sins."

We bless our children, though, which is not different, really, from the intent of this imagined baptism of baby Miranda.

Annie Dillard, in a beautifully complex and enigmatic essay about humanity's quest for the sacred, describes the baptism of another child.

Before the actual sprinkling, the priest anoints the child with oil and "repeats a gesture he says was Christ's, explaining that it symbolically opens the infant's five senses to the knowledge of God."

As I held each of my own infants in my arms, giving them their names and blessings according to the dictates of the Spirit on those days, I, too, hoped that their senses would be opened to that sacred mystery.

As this is our common hope, it is not surprising that the mystery's unraveling doesn't occur in the sole companionship of those of our particular faith.

A part of my family, for instance, is Cheyenne, as it may also be Catholic and Baptist, Methodist and Lutheran — and spiritually agnostic.

May the circle of our praying be as broad as eternity.

"If you're so smart, why ain't you rich?"

For as long as I've been at Perry Central, Tell City teachers have been working without a contract.

Naturally, I've been interested in that dispute, as I'm now interested in the chair factory dispute.

Of course, I'm not party to the inside deliberations in either case, and can't speak to the accuracy or inaccuracy of certain charges made by all four disputants.

While that is true — and acknowledging certain biases that I've developed over the years about the value of education, and that of any honest labor — I do believe that the truth of a few general ideas might be verified and tested in each of the present cases.

A friend of mine outside of teaching argues that America's social ills will not begin to be resolved until, as a nation, we're prepared to pay teachers what we now pay professional athletes.

I agree with the valuation implied: our society needs good teachers more than it needs good basketball players.

On the other hand, of course, though the exaggeration has its point, no one needs $1 million or more per year.

Surely, if there is such a thing as sin, it must be sinful to expect an annual income in the millions, while begrudging honest laborers what they fairly request in exchange for their work — which might reasonably be asked to answer, not only for their family's most basic needs, but also their modest wants.

This concept would seem to apply in both of the present cases.

While it might be argued that the current school board has few resources to throw around (hence the reluctance to increase teachers' salaries), the society at large is full of grossly affluent people who cynically withhold that wealth from relatively impoverished workers and educators.

The immediate question remains, too: whence the money to pay for lawyers and litigation, if there isn't money for the slight increases in salary that were originally requested? (I remain confused on that point.)

It also bears pointing out that the teachers remain on duty, have continued all this time to work, beyond the dictates of their non-renewed contracts.

My bias stands in their favor, then, as they go back to negotiations this week, whatever errors of judgment may be charged by some to individual teachers or their union; and despite the fact that each board member, whatever side they each come down on, is a person whose humanity I won't disparage.

Similar points may be made in favor of the strikers.

Two of them, in recent letters to the editor, make some points that seem to demand direct response.

In short: whence the money to pay security guards for what they do, and to bust the union that is viewed by workers as their legitimate voice?

Where does that money come from, if there is not enough to pay people who have been loyal workers, performing back-straining labors at 40 hours or more per week — enough, at the very least, that their families don't require public assistance?

Each side hurts itself when it engages in childish behavior, whether that be a striker "moonlighting" management or management's hired guns taunting women strikers.

The truth remains, though, that the laborer does a vital work that can't be replaced (and therefore should not be undervalued) by management.

The social Darwinist says: "If you're so smart, why ain't you rich?"

The saying contains a lie, which is that the only value in work exists in the amount of money earned, and that the greater salary is intrinsically owed to management.

Better an honest (and more egalitarian) alliance between management and labor.

What I propose has been tried in this country, and has worked, but that's another subject, and in the present climate, perhaps, a bit utopian.

A conversation with Johnny Appleseed

I was pleased to make the acquaintance the other day of one John Chapman, better known as Johnny Appleseed.

I'd missed the program that he gave to some of the elementary children the day before, but there he was at the Dogwood Festival on Saturday.

And there I was, manning the Spanish Club booth with Brian Flynn, trying to sell some chances on three grapevine wreaths that a friend of Anita's had donated.

Those of you who've followed my column know from a previous essay that Johnny Appleseed is a personal hero of mine.

I have grown up admiring his gentle nature and distinctly American pacifism.

Having met him now in person, I also have to admire his sharp frontier wit and winning humor.

He is pictured in the notices around school with a scruffy beard, but on this day was mostly clean-shaven.

His is a teasing, humorous face, one that makes children and adults (minus a few old grumps) smile in enjoyment. I liked his clean but ragged outfit, especially the floppy hat and the bare feet. When he talks to you, whether by way of narration or gentle cajolery, his tendency is to lean forward and put his face near to yours.

Some folks, less adventurous in their tastes or less prone to suspend disbelief, are reluctant to step into the history, but most are drawn in by his persistent charm.

I willingly and deliberately engaged him in talk.

I asked him to tell of an early experience in Indiana, and he told of some Hoosiers who'd told tales of him that were both untrue and unkind. I can't remember the exact thread of that gossip, which, after all these years, he seemed to find amusing.

Later I asked him about his encounters with animals. Having myself been given to conversations with grazing cattle and small rodents, I was interested in rumors that he was of a similar predilection. The fact is, he said, those stories have been stretched. It's true that he helped out some animals that had been wounded or sick, and was on healthy terms with them, but he didn't converse with them nor they with him: he wasn't crazy.

(I had to tell him that, though not certifiably crazy either, I've been known to tell some animal tales that were perhaps stretching the facts a bit. He seemed pleased to be talking with another storyteller.)

Most gratifying to me, though, was to discover what I'd never in a million years have imagined — that John Chapman speaks Spanish. A friend of his, as he tells it, one who looks a lot like him and follows him around a lot, used to live in Peru, where he worked for the Peace Corps and taught some. Later he lived in Costa Rica, but mostly in Peru.

Despite the excursion into fluent Spanish, which especially bedazzled the Spanish students who were lingering around, he was fully convincing as Johnny Appleseed, who just happened to have a gift we weren't aware of.

All the world's a stage, after all, and we but actors on it, as Shakespeare reminds us — or a character of his, in a more cynical context.

In my life, I hope to become as successful in all of the important roles that I have to assume, not least among them the role of teacher.

As for this meeting with a childhood hero, I only have one regret.

I should have bartered with him: a chance at a grapevine wreath for a handful of apple seeds.

Meteorological tales worth telling and hearing

"There are seven or eight phenomena in the world that are worth talking about," writes naturalist Annie Dillard, "and one of those is the weather."

As the other week's rain kept falling, its lightning flashing, its thunder thundering, I was inclined to agree.

"Whaddaya think of the weather?" is as good an opening line as any, and often leads to something worth telling.

Such as a story told in a novel that I recently re-read. The novel's called *All the Pretty Horses*, by Cormac McCarthy, and is a really fine read.

At book's beginning, our young protagonist's grandfather is being buried amidst a lot of Texas wind. Later, son and father sit down in a cafe and the father tells this story of a man up on the Texas Panhandle who says that, when the wind stops blowing, the chickens fall over.

A good story, that. And a powerful wind.

Exaggerated or not, such stories have the ring of truth. They're worth both the telling and the hearing. Even if they're totally fabricated, they have the power to amuse and entertain, to relieve the monotony that otherwise threatens to set in.

I was just reading some English compositions the other day, for instance, when I came on Danny Kleaving's tall tale of a recent Leopold tornado, dating to before my family's arrival in the county.

"Now, I didn't think there was such a storm in Leopold that recently," I thought as I read it, and then supposed that there could have been.

The description was so colorfully wrought, with such splendid images as the neighbor's chicken flying across the yard and slamming into a wall, that I willingly suspended disbelief — if just for a moment.

When I handed the papers back, announcing that Danny's was to be read aloud, I saw him hiding his wide, boyish grin behind his hands, and I thought to ask him if it had really happened.

It hadn't, but we all enjoyed the tale anyway. A finer one was not to be had in all the class.

There are other weather stories that a family accumulates, some more exciting than others.

Exciting is my parents' and brother's drive through a December ice storm, the width of Arkansas and length of eastern Texas from Texarkana to Houston, to visit us for Christmas.

Their safe arrival was not a foregone conclusion.

Another memory was a family camping trip into Canada with my parents and brothers, where, among other places, we visited Quebec City, which my impressionable teenage self believed to be the most beautiful and romantic city in North America.

The air was gray and misty the whole time there, but I couldn't have been more delighted. The rain suited that walled city and it was gentle enough that we could still enjoy the seeing.

Then there's the experience of Jonathan, who, since he was conscious of anything, has been fascinated by weather.

As soon as he was old enough to sit up and hold a crayon, he was imitating the colorful weather maps in the Bloomington newspaper, drawing his own maps with accompanying keys. Paris, France and Billings, Montana would appear together on the same global continent, with variations of temperature indicated by shades of color.

If we had been able to pull off a western vacation in those years, we'd have had to stop in Billings, whose only claim to fame, as far as we know, is the presence there of a weather station.

Jonathan puts a lot of stock in what weathermen say and may, if he doesn't become something else first, become one of them himself. When he wants to stay up late to catch the most recent report from Channel 32, however, I just say what I've always said before.

In the morning, stick your head out the window. There the weather awaits.

On Frito banditos and Indian outlaws

When I was younger and more impressionable than I am now, I was influenced by a Yankee entrepreneurial vision of the Mexican soul.

How many of you remember the Frito Bandito of Sixties-era commercial fame?

This was my first exposure to the chorus of the Mexican folk song "*Cielito Lindo*" — the famous "*Ay ay ay ay*" chorus, albeit in slightly distorted form. It was years before I realized that *Ay ay ay ay, I am the Fri-to Ban-di-to . . .* was not authentic.

More recently I've had to teach the correct words to Anita and the children, so that when I want to sing them, they don't intrude with that timeworn jingle.

I'm thinking of this, anyway, in the wake of Greywolf and Spiritwoman's recent visit to my English classes, where we're learning about the various contexts of persuasion. Greywolf tried to persuade us, among other things, to take a closer look at the recently popular country song "Indian Outlaw." As traditional Indians, he and his family have found the song offensive, for reasons that may be obscure to most of us who aren't traditional Indians.

In a written statement, Greywolf comments on offensive passages.

The line about the medicine man dragging another Indian around by his headband is perhaps the clearest example. Their medicine men, he explains, are their holy people, not somebody's clowns. "We respect our Holy People just as you do your Ministers and Religious Leaders," he writes. "We would never expect them to drag anyone around, nor would they."

Greywolf also cites the silly "buffalo briefs" passage. And, with all the Hollywood images that it conjures up, the light reference to "beatin' on my tom tom."

"The drum is the heartbeat of our People," Greywolf writes. "It is sacred . . . not something to be made fun of. Indian People respect the drum and honor the songs that come from the drum."

Now, that last point may be the most difficult for the non-traditional Indian to understand. How does that line make fun of the sacred?

I think Greywolf's perspective becomes clearer, though, when each of the cited passages is considered in terms of its being a part of the whole. That whole reflects a Hollywood bias that has always shown, until very recently, the Indian as outlaw. Therefore, everything about the people is distorted. Hence the discomfort — as we are uncomfortable when someone from outside of our particular faith wants to make the fool of us because of our religion.

This brings me back to the Frito Bandito, who, like another of my childhood characters, Little Black Sambo, went out of public favor while I was still growing up. The image of the lazy Mexican bandit, sleeping under his sombrero instead of working, was viewed as prejudicial.

As for me and my parents, we liked the Frito Bandito. We didn't understand the outcry about image. Weren't those complaining ethnics just being thin-skinned?

There's a lot to be said on that point, as Don Quixote often observes — more than, within the confines of this essay, I could begin to explore.

I have come to realize, anyway, that it's easy for the people wielding the image to dismiss the people it hurts as mere whiners. Nevertheless, the stereotyped Native and Mexican or

African American has real trouble in public life when he runs up against, as he does, people who believe the false image. If the image bears false witness against our neighbor, we might do well to look twice at it.

Sensitivity, not censorship, is the issue that I hear Greywolf raising.

It might be hoped that we love an ingrained image less than the flesh-and-blood neighbor who would speak to us about his legitimate experience and feelings.

On the patient wisdom of turtles

Something about the spring rains brings out the turtle population in southern Indiana. This was the case the other Sunday, the day after my and Jonathan's return from a church-organized father/son campout over in Harrison County.

It didn't rain until we'd gotten back home.

Next day, on wet roads between Leopold and English where we currently attend church, the turtles were out in force. I had been seeing them before, and have seen them since, but they seem most prevalent during and after the rains. There they are, in any case — tucked away in that impenetrable armor, fortified against attack at road's side or center, waiting stoically for one more car to pass.

~*~

Between the rain showers, Anita and I went into Tell City to see the Holocaust movie, *Schindler's List*.

That's not an easy film to watch. I personally grieved, as I always have at unconscionable injustices, great and small.

The first time I struggled was during the scene where the Polish Jews were driven out of their homes into the ghettos, preparatory to the atrocities that we know were to follow. A little child, parroting her parents' ignorant and fearful prejudices, was shouting hatefully after them: "Goodbye, Jews! Goodbye, Jews!" What could she have ever known about the guilt or innocence, in relation to her own people's suffering, of those people she mocked?

~*~

In his passionate novel of the Dust Bowl era, *The Grapes of Wrath*, John Steinbeck writes of the plight of the Okies uprooted from their ravaged soil to live a migrant's life, persecuted by fearful landowners in California.

He tells a story about a turtle trying to cross a road.

A middle-aged woman swerves to miss the turtle, who for a moment lies still within its house, then emerges again to continue the journey. Then comes a light truck, whose driver, upon seeing the turtle, swerves to hit it, sending it careening back to the side of the road from whence it had first come.

The turtle just plods back, though, its "old humorous eyes" looking ahead, its "horny beak opened a little."

The turtle is like the Joad family at novel's center, like the Jewish nation at movie's center, so persistent in one Nazi man's imagination that he's unable to let history be, instead gaining some personal redemption by buying the freedom of thousands.

~*~

I enjoyed watching the turtles on those wet pavements, and was careful not to hit any of them. I remembered the turtles I had kept as a boy. Those were like these. Seeing them brings back a wealth of memories.

I also enjoyed being out in the woods with my son, who like me, for all his faults and follies, is a good boy who doesn't really understand injustice. Sometimes he may be unjust himself, as I have been at times, but I also know his heart, which is larger than any of that. I must trust in time and in the force of a calm example to guide him right — a calm that I don't always have but that the turtles may help me to cultivate. It was good to be with him in the woods, anyway, and to sleep beside him there in our own tent.

He'd retired first. I stayed up most of the night with friends around the fire.

We played our guitars and sang songs, all the while exulting, looking up at the sky and imagining ourselves a part of the same creation as every turtle.

Recalling the rich life of a departed friend

A couple of months ago, I delivered the eulogy at my dear friend Julia Hernández's funeral.

Julia was 88 years old. She was born in Puerto Rico and came to Indiana with a daughter. I met her in Bloomington, where the daughter was doing graduate work at IU.

Julia didn't speak but a few phrases of English. While I lived in Bloomington, I was her interpreter in church.

I only interpreted words and ideas to her, though, while she interpreted a world of spirit to me, a world of goodness and faith and charity seldom experienced in this world, except in sacred story and scripture.

I'm thinking of Julia again as I finish reading Annie Dillard's essay called "Spring," seventh chapter of her Pulitzer-Prize-winning book *Pilgrim at Tinker Creek.*

Spring, meanwhile, is in full bloom in Perry County and summer very close.

The beauty of Julia's life remains as present as the newest birdsong, or the chatter of a child's first speech.

Here, with language's mystery, Annie's thoughts begin.

"When I was quite young," she writes, "I fondly imagined that all foreign languages were codes for English."

When she enrolled in high school French class, however, she discovered that language was more rich and more complex than that.

"I realized that I was going to have to learn speech all over again, word by word, one word at a time — and my dismay knew no bounds."

From that mystery of speech, anyway, she moves to the mystery of a mockingbird's song, the mockingbird whose song reverberates through her house when it sings in her chimney.

Why does the bird sing?

Some say, Annie reminds us, that it sings to mark its territory, but she and several scientists doubt that. In any case, she writes, the real question should be this: Why is the bird's song beautiful?

"This modified lizard's song welling out of the fireplace has a wild, utterly foreign music," she writes. "It becomes more and more beautiful as it becomes more and more familiar."

If the song were just to proclaim ownership, she asks, then why such richness and complexity?

"Beauty itself is the language to which we have no key," she concludes."And it could be that for beauty . . . there is no key . . . that we need to start over again, on a new continent, learning the strange syllables one by one."

The question I ask for Julia's life is this: Why was it, to everyone who knew her, so beautiful?

I recall a story that another friend tells about her.

This friend worked behind the counter in a McDonalds restaurant. Julia, after her husband died, would come in by herself, escorted perhaps by her daughter. Another elderly gentleman, a widower, would come in, too. One day he spoke to Julia, in an English incomprehensible to her, of his loneliness, and she chattered back in a Spanish that neither my friend nor the widower could understand.

Whenever they met thereafter, they would chatter on just the same, filling a bit of each other's loneliness, conscious of the music but not of the sense of each other's words.

"Sometimes," Annie Dillard writes, "birdsong seems just like the garbled speech of infants. There is a certain age at which a child looks at you in all earnestness and delivers a long, pleased speech in all the true inflections of spoken English, but with not one recognizable syllable."

I remember when Jonathan did that.

Julia's chatter was similar, the sense of it contained whole within the melody itself. Her song is beautiful because it's filled with love and innocence, with compassion and with a wisdom that comes of much living — of joy and of suffering both.

I can barely touch on it here, but few lives can have been as rich, few melodies as pure, as Julia's.

Free Leonard Peltier: "Liberty and justice for all"

A transforming experience occurred for me when I was about twelve years old, my son Jonathan's age.

I was attending a summer Bible school in Bloomington.

The organizers thought it would do a lot of good for our understanding of who our neighbor was, I suppose, if we visited a migrant labor camp in a surrounding county and glimpsed first-hand the hard reality of those people's lives.

I remember the brown-skinned children, and running with them to a creek not far from the ramshackle trailers where they lived.

I don't remember the trip's organizers' explicitly mentioning their intent, but I'm fairly sure I'd gotten the point by the time we drove away.

It didn't seem right that I should live in the lap of middle-class luxury, while those other people, as worthy of God's grace as I and my parents, had practically nothing.

Since then, I've had similar experiences.

I missed any first-hand knowledge of the activism of César Chávez for his own people, with that of Martin Luther King for American blacks, with the protests of American Indians at Wounded Knee in 1973 — but today those experiences come to life variously from printed page to screen.

In the bilingual novel *And the Earth Did Not Devour Him*, Tomás Rivera's anonymous voices tell of some migrant children whom the boss would not let go for water, lest he lose some profit. One of the children could not wait. The boss thought he'd scare him, teach him a lesson. But the bullet went carelessly through the child's head.

The fictional case mirrors the actual reality of injustice in these United States, where the history as told by the non-victor doesn't always reveal a brave picture.

The other night, for another example, I watched the video *Thunderheart*, which tells a fictional tale closely resembling events that actually transpired on our own Indian reservations in the 1970's. Thunderheart presents a good idea of the types of political and ecological concerns that were at stake in silencing Native American activism on the squalid reservations of the 1970's.

It's only within the past year that I learned about the actual case of Leonard Peltier, a Native American who's in federal prison for the deaths of two FBI agents whom the evidence suggests he did not kill. A shoot-out did occur. Leonard was involved, but in a traditional warrior's posture of defending a community of women and children from an unknown threat, and not at the close range of an assassin. Evidence is strong that the government lied in its presentation of evidence against him, and conspired with an anti-Indian judge to keep defense evidence out of trial.

A case is easily made that Peltier is in jail for political non-crimes of dissent, in violation of rights guaranteed by Constitutional amendment.

For a more complete account of the Peltier case, read Peter Matthiessen's *In the Spirit of Crazy Horse*, or see Michael Apted's documentary *Incident at Oglala*.

On June 8 and 9, anyway, the March for Justice '94 will have passed through Bedford on its way to Washington, D.C., where its representatives will seek an audience with the president. A core of marchers left Alcatraz Island, California, last February, I'm told, and will arrive in Washington by late July.

The march is for justice for Leonard (letters and petitions

are being carried), but also for justice for all Americans, in the hope that someday our democratic ideals may be extended more fully to everyone.

Windsong was to have joined the march through southwestern Indiana to Bedford. The other Greywolfs were involved in the arrangements, at Bedford, for food and shelter for the marchers.

For my part I've written, petitioning President Clinton for an executive pardon, and been joined in that activity by about half a dozen students.

As one of those students suggests in her letter, "Leonard Peltier should be free to instill hope of democracy back into the people of this country and back into the first people of this land, the Native Americans."

R is for Regal: Gallivanting with Grandma to baby brother's wedding

I'm just back from gallivanting with my grandma Mary Kroessman of Tell City. The occasion for our journeying was my little brother Kirk's June 11 wedding to Rebecca Clark, whom he'd met where they've been studying in Austin, Texas, and whose parents reside in Reno, Nevada.

Grandma and I drove up to Indianapolis on the morning of June 9, from where we flew to Reno via Columbus, Ohio, and Phoenix, Arizona.

We stayed there with my parents in a rented apartment in Incline Village, across a mountain from Reno and above Lake Tahoe, which straddles Nevada and California.

We would be there, back and forth across the mountain, for three nights and two days, returning to Indianapolis on the 12th by means of Las Vegas and Columbus, arriving back in Perry County on the morning of the 13th.

The vacation, if for its long days and short nights was not entirely restful, was at least joyful, and at last refreshing.

I was reminded in fresh ways of the deep feelings I have for my brother Kirk and my grandma Mary.

Kirk, whose middle name is Regan with a long *e* (the Mormon bishop who married him and Rebecca pronounced it with the long *a* of Reagan), was born twenty-six years ago this July in Perry County Memorial Hospital. Grandma, before departing for the big event, told Dr. Ress she was going to see the wedding of the baby he'd delivered those several years earlier.

My parents and I and my other brother, Todd, were on a stopover on our cross-country move from the Los Angeles area to Indianapolis, where Kirk would spend his first two years.

From there, he's steadily grown into the image of his second name, which in essence means kingly, or as the name sounds, regal.

That's my first impression of Kirk, anyway, as he stands before the trellis in the Clark family's backyard among the mountains surrounding Reno, on that Saturday afternoon of June 11.

He's short in stature, but entirely regal in bearing, head held high and sculpted smile as perfect as some artist's creation for a king's court. His mom, and friends who've witnessed his courtship over the past year, would describe that adoring smile as giddy, yet even in deepest infatuation it seems clothed in magisterial dignity.

His best man, Ryan, who flew west from the Chicago seminary where he's studying for the Catholic priesthood, toasted him and Rebecca in his own appropriately regal manner, at the dinner that followed the wedding. He remembered their first meeting on the El train (they were both students at Northwestern University in the Chicago suburb of Evanston), where they struck up a conversation on Plato (the Greek philosopher), Joseph Smith (the Mormon prophet), and R.E.M. (the rock group) — in classical Latin.

I, who have grown to respect Kirk so much for his intelligence and wit, and for his brotherly counsel and conversation even at a distance, was moved by Ryan's toast: that the two lovers be blessed with children who are "fruit and symbol" of that true love — which, if I may add a phrase, is both mortal and divine.

All of this said, in any case, I must add that my feelings for Kirk are no deeper than what I felt at this time for my grandma, doting companion of our recent travels. The regal quality that pervades Kirk's character is at least in part an inheritance from her, as is also much that I recognize in my own character.

Kirk's assurance of things (which in some degree I lack) comes from Dad, whose rise from country boy to government and civil service reveals a great confidence in his own decisions and judgment.

I have been less sure of myself at almost all times, more given to apologies and second-guessing.

I recognize a touch of that in my grandma, who humbly thanks me for any little care shown her, as if she owed me for it. She, who had helped Mom raise me, nurture me — change my diapers (before Dad moved us out to Arizona, then California). Behind that uncertainty — her reluctance to presume on any other person, or to claim a clear understanding of certain problems and paradoxes of our existence — is the bearing and dignity that we often call *class*.

It's that same class that I recognize in the stories she tells, for instance, of my great-grandfather, Emil Kroessman, who during Depression years ran Fischer Chair Company with dignity and compassion.

It's the same class that I've recognized in Kirk.

God bless him and Rebecca now in their new life together.

On heroes, cowboys, and Indians

My heroes, as I was growing up, were not, in fact, always cowboys. The mystique of the American cowboy, though, has dogged me from birth, when my mother named me for a TV parody of one — James Garner's quick-smiling, smooth-talking Bret Maverick.(In an uncharacteristic fit of extravagance that must have been influenced, unconsciously, by Maverick's penchant for gambling, Mom abandoned her usual frugality and added an extra *t*.)

I only have the vaguest memories of that show, anyway, and until recently, when I gambled away three quarters in a Nevada casino (for a scandalous return of one hundred), I'd never thought of myself as much of a maverick.

I was a tame child, for the most part, indulging myself only in the usual rowdy games — which of course included army, as well as cowboys and Indians. I wore, alternately, Stetson hat and coonskin cap. And, while living out west with my parents, I occasionally attended the rodeo.

Anyway, even since losing what active interest I'd ever had in the cowboy experience, the mystique has been kept alive for me in certain bits of music and literature.

I've mentioned before in this column, for instance, Cormac McCarthy's trailblazing novel in English and Spanish, *All the Pretty Horses*. Whether we call some of its characters cowboys or the more rugged *vaqueros* (herders of *vacas*, or cows), that narrative brilliantly evokes the reality and romance of a true western landscape, without indulging in any of the standard stereotypes.

In high school I listened to James Taylor, who, in his classic ballad "Sweet Baby James" (which still soothes me after all these years), must be responding to that mystique of our mythical "wild west" as it had spoken to him.

My favorite Garth Brooks songs are also his quiet *vaquero* ballads — "Night Rider's Lament," for instance, and the one simply called "The Cowboy Song."

What attracts me to Garth's ballads, in particular, is that they seem to capture something of the pure appeal of a rugged past, for a moment innocent of the general run of rhinestone cowboys and country singers who cash in on it — innocent, even, of John Wayne's Hollywood mythologizing.

John Wayne's cowboy is, in fact, myth, as is the pre-*Dances with Wolves* Indian of countless movies and cartoons.

Behind the myth is the reality. Sometimes, by parodying the one, we come closer to the other.

Such is the case, I think, with the movie *Maverick*, which, out of curiosity about the TV series that inspired it, and that also inspired my naming, I went on a recent Saturday to see.

I can't say how it compares to the original, nor the original to it, but I can say what seems good to me about the movie, which above all strikes me as having produced more than ample laughs without also being painfully stupid. I vaguely recall a *TV Guide* critic's complaint that the movie, as a parody of a parody, was pushing its luck with the gags, but to me it worked effectively on that level of an original parody.

I didn't miss the deliberate humor of casting old Maverick against new (James Garner against Mel Gibson), nor the twist that the movie's ending rides on, but I rather thought all of that just added to the fun.

Jodie Foster, who rounds out the movie's trio of lovable rogues, is also great fun to watch, but I most enjoyed the casting of Native American Graham Green (*Dances with Wolves*,

Thunderheart, Northern Exposure) in the role of Maverick's Indian friend and cohort.

The sequence where Maverick joins up with this group of authentic-looking Indians (he speaks their language, and is owed money by the one played by Greene) is uproariously funny.

This is the heart of parody. The mock reality of authentic 19th-century Indian life is played off Hollywood stereotypes, as the whole Maverick persona is played off the stylized images that preceded it.

To bring the parody fully into the 20th century, in any case, I recommend the video *Raising Arizona*, which hilariously spoofs old-time westerns by bringing them face to face with the domesticity of our contemporary, convenience-store society. It has no Indians in it, but a variety of other sorts, including the unlikeliest of western heroes and the baddest of frontier bad men.

You may never look at John Wayne in quite the same way.

"Your huddled masses yearning to breathe free"

This Fourth of July, as the family gears up for its first Independence Day excursion to Holiday World, I'm drawn to some American words that I hope will put the occasion in a true perspective. I open the pages of *The American Reader*, edited by Diane Ravitch.

The fireworks will come later, and, sandwiched between them and these words, the various rides and amusements that Holiday World offers. But it would seem almost sacrilege to enjoy the spectacle without first giving thought to a driving motivation behind it — a universal hope for genuine liberty contained, for instance, in these words, both celebratory and critical.

We are all acquainted with the Declaration of Independence, penned in its original draft by Thomas Jefferson, amended by the Continental Congress.

"We hold these truths to be self-evident, that all men [and women] are created equal . . . endowed by their Creator with certain inalienable Rights. . . ."

These rights are secured, according to Jefferson, by governments, which obtain their powers "from the consent of the governed" and may be overthrown if they become abusive of those individual rights.

These words are well-known. Less acknowledged, if not infrequently discussed, is our own conservative government's quickness — in contradiction to Jefferson's revolutionary dictum about the casting off of abusive governments — to put down, in the interest of its own economic security, foreign (or domestic) revolts against clear abuses.

(Such was the case when, in Nicaragua earlier this century, we overthrew one nationalist leader, contributed to the martyrdom and deification of another, and sustained over decades the petty tyranny of Anastasio Somoza; such has also been true on our own Indian reservations, where countless murders of activist Indians go uninvestigated, while the self-defense shooting of two FBI agents is severely and feloniously prosecuted.)

None of which, of itself, speaks against the rightness of Jefferson's words, which we rightly celebrate.

We are justly inspired, likewise, by the words of Emma Lazarus, whose 1883 poem announces the hope and symbolism of the yet-to-be unveiled Statue of Liberty.

"Give me your tired, your poor,
Your huddled masses yearning to breathe free,
The wretched refuse of your teeming shore.
Send these, the homeless, tempest-tost to me,
I lift my lamp beside the golden door!"

The actual reception of America's immigrant poor, as the poet well knew, was seldom so embracing. Yet in contrast to the brutal impoverishments of sweatshops and indentured servitudes were successes, small and large, of which the Swiss Colonization Society's 1858 founding of Tell City (my own forebears being present) was one.

So it's understandable when, in church on the Sunday before the Fourth, we sing patriotic songs, and give thanks for the privileges of living in a land where we are free, for instance, to worship according to the dictates of our own conscience.

Yet when the freedom of any brother or sister is abridged, as when, in Indiana, Native American ceremonies and visitations to prison inmates are forbidden (while gospel-sings and visitations of Christian ministers are allowed), then my own privilege feels incomplete.

It is in this context that I understand the words of Frederick Douglass, escaped and illegally educated slave, to an Independence Day crowd in 1852.

"This Fourth of July is yours, not mine. You may rejoice, I must mourn. To drag a man in fetters into the grand illuminated temple of liberty, and call upon him to join you in joyous anthems, were inhuman mockery and sacrilegious irony."

To acknowledge such faults, past or present, is not to denigrate what should be truly celebrated. It is just to remind us, more forcefully than the fireworks alone can do, of the roots of our own rebellion, when Thomas Jefferson penned those truly radical words about human rights and dignity.

Camping: Answering the call of the wild

As I write these words tonight, our children are asleep outside in the new tents we set up for them, preparatory to our family's first-ever camping trip.

Stephanie, who's never slept outside, was excited until the lights went out. We turned on the porch light, then, and let her take courage from Nadina. (Jonathan, meanwhile, off in a tent of his own, was dozing; the larger tent between his and the girls' was awaiting the weekend and the woods, where Anita and I will finally sleep in it.)

So you see that we're new at this.

I'd camped before with my parents. Anita had camped with hers, too, but all of that was long ago. Neither of us was confident, until this last spring when I got the urge really strong, of camping on our own, and even then Anita made me settle for a more tentative beginning than the Big Western Vacation I'd mapped out so we could take in Kirk's wedding.

We didn't all make it to the wedding, but that was never the real impetus behind my urge to camp.

When I was up to Bloomington this spring, visiting with some friends, I mentioned this resurgent call of the wild, to which this time I intended to respond.

Maybe the question had been what I had in mind for the summer, and I answered that, among other things, I thought I would take up camping.

"Why?" Martha asked simply.

Her arms were folded in front of her, and she brought one hand thoughtfully to her chin. Puzzlement was written all over her face.

I remembered that, when some of our more zealous Mormon compatriots used to talk, romantically, of hiking like Boy Scouts to Missouri (where in their imaginations they'd re-inherit a physical Zion abandoned to 19th-century persecutions), Martha humorously proclaimed that they could march if they wanted, but she'd be going first class — by plane.

Knowing her preferences in respect to sleeping outdoors, then, I wasn't sure how to explain my reasons to her.

"I just want to," I must have said — or something just as stupid as that.

Naturalist Terry Tempest Williams, anyway, in her 1994 book *An Unspoken Hunger*, tells a story that may be pertinent, of a seminar that turned into a camping trip into the Southwestern landscape of the Palo Duro Canyon. She had been invited to speak (again to a group of Mormons, of which she is one) on the spirituality of nature.

As they settled in there, and she began to read from scripture, some coyotes began to howl.

"God's dogs," she writes simply, adding that she'd been moved to howl with them. When she invited the congregation to do likewise, they did: "Mormons and coyotes, united together in a desert hallelujah chorus!"

I like the story. I admit I wouldn't mind howling, too, with our own Perry County coyotes.

In tardy answer to Martha's question, then, I guess something of this is what draws me to the woods. I regret the practical intimacy I've lost, in the sometimes quiet desperation of my adult life, with God's multitudinous creations, which, like us, exist in physical space.

In fact, I think Williams is right when she suggests, in her book, a real relationship between humanity's lack of intimacy with itself and with the land. We cut ourselves off, to varying degrees, from our wild, holy nature as part of God's creation.

Still, I won't ask Martha to flock into the woods with my family and me. I doubt it's necessary. But I do believe a heightened awareness of nature's spirituality, and humanity's place and responsibility within it, might help to redeem us all from whatever desperations we face.

On the tendency to loneliness and melancholy

"A tendency to melancholy," Abraham Lincoln is reported to have observed, "is a misfortune, not a fault."

The word itself, derived from the Old French, is stressed on its first syllable. The first two syllables together, *mel-on*, sound like a breakfast fruit; the last two, *col-lie*, like a type of long-haired dog. This, anyway, is how it's come down to us; in poetic forms (the *h* has always been silent) it used to be stressed on its second or fourth syllable (*Oxford English Dictionary*).

I like the word, anyway, having always found it richer, more flavorful, than *depression* or *depressed*, which we hear more commonly today.

Depression, in any case, is only part of my conception of melancholy, which I shall try to reveal here in some of its broader significance.

Thus, I am indebted to our sixteenth president, whose own frequent melancholy, like mine, helped shape his soul. Today, he'd be kept from that office by it; his sometimes mournful disposition would be trumpeted as psychological unsteadiness, moral depth thus traded for superficial cheer or bluster.

Melancholy, in any case, is infinitely more than a psychological or mental disorder; it may just as well lead to wisdom as to ruin.

The Spanish writer Cervantes understood this when he wrote about his mournful knight, Don Quixote, who'd at last died of his particular melancholy, these words of adulation: "he had the fortune in his age / to live a fool and die a sage" (Walter Starkie's translation).

There is, of course, no particular virtue in death by melancholy, nor would I have anyone read into these words any depressed glorification of a romantic tendency to suicide.

Don Quixote, for his part, had taken his own brooding, about man's inhumanity to man, for instance, and sallied forth quite alive, full of love and vigor. His supposed madness, his chasing after windmills as if they were evil giants and he the knight in shining armor destined to rid the world of them, was essentially a hopeful man's effort to bring sense to what to him seemed senseless.

He was misguided only in the particulars; at last he acknowledged that misguidedness, admitting the limitations of his mortality and dying sad but wise, a part of him still knowing, I want to believe, that the spirit of his quest had always been right.

I speak of this literary fiction as if he were a real man, anyway, because I think the point's in the comparison. His melancholy brooding and his mad, fanciful antics represent the spirit-yearning part of our nature, and his practical sidekick Sancho Panza represents our mortal needs and limitations; in effect, we need to be Quixote and Panza in one, our basic grounding in necessity leavened by a dash of idealism.

The word itself, *melancholy*, seems to me a product of that idealism, which, when confronted now and again with the harshness of our immediate human destiny, produces a bit of the gloominess or depression of spirits that characterizes a melancholy soul, or a state of melancholy.

The word exists, of course, as both noun and adjective, the adjectival uses ("he's a melancholy soul") deriving from the substantive uses of the noun ("he's given to frequent bouts of melancholy").

The noun has originally to do with a supposed disease, physical and mental, characterized by fits of sullen, violent anger, at the time thought to be caused by the body's overproduction of black bile and referred to then as melancholia. In later usage, the melancholy person was mournful but not necessarily violent, and it became fashionable for the princely or artistic man to strike a melancholy pose, symbol of real or feigned enlightenment (*OED*).

The understanding of such phenomena has progressed far from those early suspicions about black bile, to the point that, today, medical science claims particular knowledge about chemical sources of chronic depression, and has produced drugs to counter its debilitating effects.

Chronic depression such as leads people to thoughts of suicide might well be treated, then, with the best that our doctors can offer, but let's not forget the spiritual secrets that may also lie within a broad definition of melancholy, which perhaps shouldn't be entirely forsaken.

Part of this, I think, is related to a parallel condition called loneliness, which may just as well happen to a person when he's in a crowd as alone.

"My loneliness is deep and incurable," writes the poet-singer Woody Guthrie. "I ache and hurt inside," he adds, "because the world needs so much fixin'."

Yet in that loneliness — that melancholy — it's not despair he finds, but his own poet's yearning for peace; his practical sense of what it takes to survive in a mortal world is leavened by that spiritual quest, quixotic at its core, that, after all, might exalt us.

"Thank the Lord for loneliness," Woody says at last.

And for melancholy, too, which, despite its heaviness, may be more than misfortune — and certainly isn't a fault.

A reluctant testimonial for call-waiting

On the long drive home the other evening from Jasper, where I've just finished teaching a summer class in college composition, I was listening to 92.5 WBKR's country music request program called "Cryin', Lovin', Leavin', or Lookin'?"

The young man requesting a song was having trouble; an annoying clicking sound kept interrupting his voice.

"Oh," said the disc jockey after a couple of those interruptions, "you've got call-waiting, don't you?"

"Yeah," the frustrated caller answered, "and it's beginning to suck."

I understood his feelings. I'd been similarly irritated the first time we added call-waiting to our service. Whenever my conversations were interrupted by that incessant clicking, I'd become paralyzed and start stuttering, no longer capable of intelligent discourse with the person then on the line, let alone of taking the necessary steps to find out who was trying to break in. I persuaded Anita to cancel.

Recently, though, without my knowledge, she added the service again. She called the phone company in the morning and told me in the afternoon. I complained, but this time there's no question it will stay. That very evening we had need of it, and Anita, of course, wasn't slow to say she'd told me so.

It was a Monday or a Wednesday, I don't recall which. This time I was driving *to* Jasper for the evening class. As fortune would have it, though, I didn't make it, and when I finally did make it to a phone to call Anita, it was thanks to call-waiting that I got through.

When I did get through, about twenty minutes after I was to have begun my class, her voice was choked. "Where have you been?" she asked, echoing the Grammy-winning question that Kathy Mattea sang a few years ago.

The thing was, I'd blown out a tire just north of Ferdinand on 162. I'd tried to use my useless jack to replace the tire and then tried to call an auto repair place from the self-serve Marathon station I'd limped back to. No one answered; I assumed they were too busy and just not answering the phone.

So I set off on foot and walked the length of Ferdinand only to discover that the place was closed not more than half an hour before I knocked at their doors.

By the time I got back toward the car and called collect from a grocery store pay phone, a secretary from the school had already called Anita, as I was afraid would have happened. Anita had been trying to recall details about the car and what I'd been wearing, and wondering how she was going to tell my parents, so close on the heel of their youngest son's wedding, of their eldest son's death. She'd been doing that when I called; I owe my reaching her then to an annoying clicking.

I was deeply distressed for the rest of the evening, more on account of the grief I'd caused the girl who loved me than of the blown tire or missed class.

I called 911, anyway, and the policeman found my jack as useless as I had. He went for a better one and, between the two of us, we did the job. Next day I went to Tell City Tire and replaced both the temporary and, for good measure, the last of my old tires.

I've had no more tire trouble since then, but I have been stopped on the road; this, as fortune would have it, was on a Monday evening as I was headed again to Jasper.

This time I'd been adding oil and water to the car before dropping Jonathan and Nadina at Perry Central's pre-band camp. I had time to spare to get to Jasper, but was a little behind in getting the kids to the school. In my rush, I forgot to secure the radiator cap. When the temperature light came on about a mile north of Michael's Country Mart, I knew something was wrong; when I opened the hood and saw the cap sitting where I'd left it, green liquid bubbling everywhere except where it belonged, I knew what was wrong.

I took a rag and cleaned up the mess as best I could, then crossed the road and started walking toward Michael's. About the third vehicle that passed me put on its right turn signal and stopped. It turned out to be my former Spanish student, Stan Hubert and his friend, Murray Labhart, homeward bound from their work and covered in dry cement.

They gave me a lift and I bought some coolant, later returning to the store and refilling the container with water. That did the job; the car started and I made it in time to class. I'd enjoyed some pleasant conversation in the bargain and had someone call Anita in case I might have run a little late.

Call-waiting wasn't a factor then, as far as I know, but I suppose in Anita's mind the incident still underlined the fact that it had been needed once when I was on the road, and might be needed again.

Some things become unarguable. I'm resigned. Just don't expect me to react coherently if you should be talking with me on the phone when I hear that ungodly clicking.

Humiliation: Memories of driver's training

I was in town a while ago, trying to squeeze into a narrow space between two cars on Main Street, when a conversation occurred that brought me all the way back to driver's training at Edgewood High School in Ellettsville.

"Park there," Anita ordered. "Do you think you can fit?"

I pulled up to where the nose of my vehicle was about even with the steering wheel in front of my desired spot and began to back in, swinging the back of my car to the right.

"Dad hates parallel parking," Anita observed, to which Jonathan, remembering some earlier conversation in which I'd participated, asked, "Oh, is that why he almost didn't get his driver's license?"

That's the short of it, as I'd observed a few days earlier when, for the sake of brevity, I'd just nose-dived into a spot and left the rear-end sticking out while Anita ran a sixty-second errand. This time we were going to be longer than that, so I decided to do it right; with a little repositioning, forward and backward, I succeeded.

That's the short of it, anyway. The long of it is a more complicated matter, going back to when I took driver's training about twenty years ago at Edgewood High School from an irascible old codger who, for the sake of not getting sued, I'll just call Mr. E.

Mr. E was not noted for his patience. I even think he rather disliked children, given the stories that I've heard told on him, none of which, based on that summer's experience, I find hard to believe. We had just moved to Ellettsville, so I'd never had him where he taught at the junior high. My brother Todd came up after me, though, and told me some horrible tales, such as the day Mr. E took one look at a girl — she hadn't said a word — and proclaimed, "God, you're ugly!"

(Time and profession have taught me to be skeptical of many of the tales children tell on their teachers, but experience also reminds me that in some cases the tales are true; I also know something about my brother at the time and when he was truth-telling or lying.)

Anyway, I digress. This was my first summer in Ellettsville and Mr. E was my driving instructor. I got A's in class and a no-waiver on the road, which meant that, as he put it, he could not "in good conscience put me out on the road where I might kill someone."

The experience of driving with him was well-captured in a creative writing paragraph I wrote a couple years later for Margaret Meadors, a high school teacher who today is my friend. I was supposed to write about an experience that shows a particular emotion that words alone could not describe.

"I'm at the wheel," I wrote. "The driving is smooth. My instructor isn't yelling at me. There must be some mistake. This is a dream. Wait, here's a turn. I made it, but no. I did something wrong. He's yelling again. What the devil did I think I was doing? Didn't I see that sign? Maximum speed 25? I was going at least 35! Did I want to kill him? Sorry. I was slowing down, just not fast enough. Don't talk back! That's not good enough! Sorry's no good when he's laid up in the hospital! What? There I go again! Don't I know any traffic rules? What lane do I think I'm in? My head is spinning. I can't think. Stop yelling. Shut up! Don't I have any respect for him? Good grief, I've done it again! Don't I care? Am I trying to kill him? Get off the road! He's had enough! I'm not worth his life! He's going to call my parents! He doesn't care if I come back or not! My thoughts are in chaos. I'm a disgrace. I've blown it. My whole body is shaking. I barely get the car off the road without giving him an ulcer. What do the other guys think? They must think I'm a fool. What will Mom and Dad say? I'm humiliated. Ashamed. I can't hide the tears. Why do I need to drive, anyway?"

Miss Meadors gave me an A for content and an A for mechanics. She wrote this note: "You certainly chose the right subject. Everyone reacted to your paragraph."

My journal for that date tells me that one girl in the class commented, after the reading: "You know, that sounds just like Mr. E."

So it wasn't just me.

When I did finally go for my license, anyway — I was too terrified for months after that summer's training — it was because I didn't want my dad to drive me and my date to the prom. I was seventeen years old by then. I nervously went out on the road with a kindly lady who, after we were finished, asked me if I hadn't gotten much practice at parallel parking.

"My teacher wouldn't let me do it the second time," I said. "I made him nervous."

"Well, I'll go ahead and give you your license," she said, "but you have to promise me that you'll go out on some country road and practice parallel parking some more."

I thanked her for that, and I promised. Sorry to confess that my nerves kept me from doing so, however; instead I'd just go blocks out of my way to find a spot that was wide enough that I didn't have to worry about backing into it.

All these years later I still get cold chills and have to be mildly sedated whenever I think about Mr. E. Just writing these few lines right now has gotten me to seriously shaking.

Now I'm fairly certain, from my conversations with Kenny LaGrange out at Perry Central, that he's a much calmer driving teacher than my own Mr. E was. God bless him for it. I hope his students fully appreciate what he doesn't put them through.

"Now that the buffalo's gone": Why I joined the Indiana Indian Movement

My first acquaintance with Greywolf came about because of my teaching Spanish. I was going into my second year at Perry Central when he moved into the county and his second daughter, Moonstar, quietly entered my class; from there, somehow, a rich and loving friendship grew up between our families.

Grandfather, as they would call Him, works in mysterious ways. How wondrous the paths that brought those families together!

Love, anyway, such as we (and I hope all of you) have experienced, is something that starts and ends with the meeting of particulars. Generalized, separated from an immediate human context, love amounts at best to a possibility, at worst an illusion.

"I must admit," says Ivan, for example, in Dostoevsky's famous novel *The Brothers Karamazov*, "I have never understood how it was possible to love one's neighbors. And I mean precisely one's neighbors, because I can conceive of the possibility of loving those who are far away."

It's been from far away, as a matter of fact, that much of immigrant America has loved the first Americans, the noble savages of Longfellow's *Hiawatha*, a book that, for all of its questionable assumptions about European cultural and religious superiority, I still deeply cherish for its deeper visions.

That's been our national tendency, though. This is observably true; test it. How often do folks say they're sickened by the atrocities our people committed against Indians in past

centuries, then balk when contemporary Indians talk of
contemporary claims?

When I was a young boy and would occasionally regale my
mother with my voice and guitar, I used to sing a Sixties folk
song, "Now that the Buffalo's Gone," by Canadian-Indian Buffy
Sainte-Marie. She's still around, though not well-played and
often suppressed; her latest tape contains a song called "Bury
My Heart at Wounded Knee," and, according to the guy in
Corydon who sold it to me, has been confiscated in two states
for its political content — and this in the land of the free!

In "Now that the Buffalo's Gone," which, to help keep it
from oblivion, I've recently re-learned, she addresses herself to
those who, claiming for themselves a little bit of Indian blood,
pay lip service to sorrowing over the wrongs committed against
them.

In one verse, responding to one of the first arguments we
always hear against contemporary claims, she sings:

> *When a war between nations is lost*
> *The loser we know pays the cost*
> *But even when Germany fell to your hands*
> *Consider dear lady, consider dear man*
> *You left them their pride and you left them their land*
> *And what have you done to these ones?*

Then, after naming contemporary instances where the
government is still taking Indian lands, establishing it not as
a past but also a current problem, she says: "It's here and it's now
you must help us, dear man / Now that the buffalo's gone."

In the here and now of southern Indiana, as I've
encountered and come to love this one family, those words
have come back to me. These peoples' concerns, as they
touch on the very survival of their traditional ways and wisdoms,
seem more vital to me than anything; if immigrant,
melting-pot America takes all Indian possessions, physical
and spiritual, saying that, to exist, the Indians must first change

until they act and feel like us, they will, in important ways, cease to exist.

A passage of my Mormon scripture urges that we stand with those we love, that we be willing to "bear one another's burdens, that they may be light"; that we "mourn with those that mourn"; "comfort those that stand in need of comfort"; "that we stand with them at all times as a witness of God."

This, I think, is nothing so hard to do, and, whether we're taught to call Him Father or Grandfather, it's the same God who all of us witness; if to exist in this nation my Indian brothers and sisters must stop worshiping the old way that their conscience dictates, then our trumpeting of religious freedom is dishonest.

These, in any case, are some of the reasons that, while I don't claim a single drop of Indian blood, I've recently joined Greywolf and his family in the newly founded Indiana Indian Movement, whose members are united in their support of such important issues as religious freedom, reburial and repatriation of their dead, and education toward a tolerance and an understanding that's inclusive of Indian and non-Indian alike.

What I help them address now out of love, someone else might hear, if for no better reason, out of self-interest; the freedoms that we deny another people may as well be denied of us tomorrow.

Yes, Virginia, I was at Woodstock in '69

"Some came to sing, some came to pray.
Some came to keep the dark away.
             Melanie Safka, from Candles in the Rain

Jonathan was saying to me how he wished we had MTV at least for August so he could tune in to the actual performance of Woodstock '94, not just Letterman's stupid reports from the scene.

I had to sympathize; then it occurred to me that I'd probably never told him about my having been at the original Woodstock twenty-five years ago; needless to say, I was quick to remedy the situation.

I'm surprised I hadn't gotten around to this sooner, since my students, to whom I'm ever-so-dated, are frequently asking such questions as these:

"Were you a hippie, Mr. Sanders?"

"Were you at Woodstock, Mr. Sanders?"

This must all be fairly obvious since, despite the occasional absence of beads, I've long worn a beard and sandals. As a result of my wearing them to school, in fact, some students have taken to calling me Mr. Sandals.

"*Señor Sandalia, ¿fuiste en tal entonces a Woodstock?*"

"*Sí, señor* or *señorita*, in that long ago time I surely did go, though I was not quite eleven years old and my mama didn't know. . . ."

You don't believe me? Permit me to explain.

We had been living back in Indiana for about a year, after a stint in Arizona and California, when things got kind of strange at our suburban Indianapolis home. I don't wish to cause my good mother any embarrassment, but she was kind of distracted then — by the crazy woman next door who kept telling her what it was going to be like when she turned thirty ("Don't trust anyone over thirty," some Beatle once said; "they'll go all wacky on you").

It was easy to slip away for about a week, in any case; I suppose some neighborhood kid sat my place for me at the table, and, things being what they were, no adult in the home really noticed. I returned a few days later in a psychedelic Volkswagen van, with a bunch of teenagers and a couple of young adults who were really quite responsible, for hippies.

This would have surprised my mom, who had only seen images of wacko-sordid types of hippies in the media, though she did like the guy who taught me guitar a few years later and who, beardless and with hair not so long at all, didn't look the stereotyped role.

Not that I want to glorify that era, as if it weren't, just like any other, filled with pain and hypocrisy and stupidity, at Woodstock as well as in the Pentagon.

A lot of those hippies and activists and rebels sold out, after all, and surely some were only pretending, anyway. That doesn't mean that everyone pretended, though, or sold out, nor that the questions asked were wrong just because people didn't always find right answers.

There were excesses at Woodstock, no doubt, in the area of drugs and free sex and a lot of other things, but that's only part of the story; fortunately, since I traveled with people who did nothing weirder than dance and hug each other and tie-dye shirts, I can counter some of the bad press.

One of the adults in my group was a blond-haired ecologist; I'm reminded of her today by a thoughtful student of mine who once rebuked me for not photocopying on both sides of the paper, and who I think was growing up with the right questions in her heart.

This hippie ecologist didn't smoke anything and drank nothing stronger than tea, and she had a book, called *Black Elk Speaks*, from which we read some together, and which came to mean a lot to certain members of the Woodstock generation.

It's a great and important book, reminding us of some of the observations that American Indians have been making about our wasteful, competitive, greedy society since we first started breaking treaties and destroying environmental balances.

Whether they all meant it or not, the Woodstock generation was asking the same questions about our material culture that those Indians had been posing all along; don't blame them if they couldn't overcome the odds, or if in some respect they messed up and, like everyone else, confused the answers.

My ecologist friend thought a lot of Melanie's songs, at least some of them. She liked the song called "Peace Will Come," and wished it would have come before her big brother went away to die in Vietnam. She liked "Beautiful People," and wanted to be one, the kind you can lean on out of the darkness, to sing or to pray.

She wanted to restore the broken hoop of Indian peoples, and the childhood hopes of children generally, who were afraid of real-life demons that they still encounter outside of storybooks.

She was kind of idealistic, in short, and not very practical, but maybe that's not so bad. We could use a dose of Sixties idealism today — not the sort that spat on your cousin who went off to war, but the kind that wished he would come back. And no one have to go again.

Can it really be so bad to be an idealist of that sort?

And, anyway, she got me home safely without my mom ever noticing I'd been gone. And I still had my innocence, one more thing of which we could use a little today.

Afterword

How I stumbled into writing these essays for the *Tell City News* is related in my first report, in April of 1992, from the heart of Leopold. The gist of it is that, more or less on a whim, I answered the ad for a rural-news correspondent. Aside from the other reasons stated in that introductory essay, I also undoubtedly considered that it would be as good a way as any to establish my credentials for a future column.

That transformation came more quickly than I had anticipated, short months after my modest beginning and before the paper transformed itself, in November of the same year, from the *Tell City* to the *Perry County News*. From the beginning, in any case, these essays immediately became my principal outlet as a writer for roughly the next two and a half years — a source of much pleasure for me and, at least so I was told, for a fair portion of the reading public.

What I did not explain, in my capacity as either columnist or correspondent, was the precise origin of that little conceit of the talking (and poeticizing) cows that runs through numerous of the essays. As most nearly hinted at in the title piece, it does originate in the Spanish classroom, though more particularly in my annual routine of whipping out guitar and initiating beginning students into the gentle mysteries of Spanish pronunciation: by means of a traditional children's vowel-substitution song (think of "Apples and Bananas," if that helps):

La mar estaba serena, serena estaba la mar . . .
("The sea was serene, serene was the sea . . .")

The cows came in when we arrived at the vowel *u*, which in Spanish is pronounced like the *oo* in *moo*: *Lu muuuur u-stuuuu-bu su-ruuuu-nu . . .*

What can I say? I made a f*ooo*l of myself (anything to amuse my young charges and stimulate learning!). Who knows whether it was the *muuuu* sound itself, the thought of me out in the fields teaching the song to Maurice Edwards's cows, or the shape of my protruding lips when I made the sound that excited such an animated response from my students.

Another thread that runs through several essays and bears mentioning here concerns the Greywolf family and the Native American Indian ways into which they were initiating me. The larger story of my encounter with the Greywolfs and their Indiana Indian Movement, which ended in a darker place than I had anticipated, is related in my memoir "Dancing with Coyote," which appeared in the no-longer-functioning online journal *Tertulia Magazine*. Perhaps at some future moment I will re-publish (or otherwise re-visit) that story in a different format; but certainly, in this age of the Standing Rock protest, the Dakota Access Pipeline, Black Lives Matter, and climate change with its newly-empowered deniers, the issues remain fiercely pertinent.

The essays selected here from the number originally published are the best or most essential of them, in my view, and for the most part are presented in chronological order. This has seemed preferable to a more topical organization, since so much of the essays' flavor proceeds from the interplay between and among them, an interplay that depends on a collective digressiveness not unlike the only-apparently accidental flow of idea and incident within any one of the pieces themselves. Otherwise, without altering the chronological order, I have moved the Albertine Gleeson essay up to the end of that first section since, though technically it was the first to appear under my headshot and byline, I was still the rural-news guy when I wrote it.

The only exception to this rule is my placing of the last two essays in front of the then-controversial Woodstock piece that chronologically preceded them. This placement seems appropriate, given the hullabaloo of that moment, which led to the column's demise and thus elevates it in historical significance; though, in any case, I think it merits that preferential placement by virtue of its own, shall I say, *literary* design and content.

But therein lay the problem: a literary design whose truth, unbeknownst to the editorial staff, was more symbolic than factual. I was telling a tall tale, in other words, and was pleasantly amused when a friend of my wife's called to settle a dispute with her husband: did I, or did I not (as she argued), at the age of not-yet eleven and without my parents' missing me, attend the original Woodstock?

Sometime after Anita told me that story, I sat down to write a follow-up essay, good-humoredly explaining the method to my madness. To be brief: the made-up tale was only the scaffolding upon which the ideas themselves were hung, a way of getting at those ideas. And, given the broad hints that I dropped in this telling, as well as in a range of earlier essays — my conversations with the so-called "lower" animals, most obviously, but also the rather unlikely conversations with the fictitious Braulio and Tasha, exiles, respectively, from the generals' Argentina and the former Soviet Union — given all these signs, I had thought that I was safely within my poetic license as I spun the playful tale.

This was common practice among columnists, after all, who did not operate under the same standard as the *mere* journalists who reported and sometimes interpreted the day's actual news; and, to seal the argument, I cited a syndicated columnist of much renown — Russell Baker, whose "Observer" column graced the pages of the Sunday edition of the *New York Times* — who occasionally used the device of a fictional taxi driver to help him explore the intricacies of his topic.

Suffice it to say that the editor, for whatever reasons, did not buy that line of thought. She required, in place of the essay already submitted, an apology that in translation dripped more of sarcasm than of contrition; which swiftly led, if I may dispense with further detail and cut to the chase, to the severance of our professional relationship. "Talk of the County" was to be no more. I felt something like Edgar Allan Poe's bewildered narrator, driven mad by the persistent "Nevermore!" of his lugubrious raven.

In retrospect, though I can't help thinking the whole kerfuffle over that essay was overblown, I can see that my previous nitpicking with the staff over a handful of minor edits (tactfully, I had thought, woven into the charming patter of subsequent essays) just might have been a tad insufferable, not to say obnoxious. Out of respect, then, and by way of tardy apology (as much, perhaps, as for personal embarrassment), I have pruned any offending passage that might otherwise have found its way into this collection.

Aside from the occasional more substantive edit of these re-visited texts — for clarification or other judicious improvement and, in at least one notable instance, to repair the transition made necessary by the chopping off of offending parts — any additional changes tend to be corrections of some stray misspelling or other small imperfection, as well as some standardization of style and forms. Also, the "Rural News" essays (which originally appeared, without headline, beneath my name, mailing address, and phone number) have new titles; and the "Talk of the County" headlines, likewise, are either edited or completely altered for this book. Otherwise, the texts are essentially the same as they were when first published.

It is my hope that, retrieved from obscurity and presented to a temporally and geographically expanded audience, they will please old readers and new alike; and that, in doing so, they might also enlighten — and awaken, given their increasing turn toward the more deeply philosophical and even political.

Tell City, Indiana
June 2017

About the Author

Brett Alan Sanders is a literary translator, writer, and retired teacher living in Tell City, Indiana. Between 1991 and 2013 he taught Spanish and English at Perry Central Jr.-Sr. High School where, starting in the 2004-05 school year, he also sponsored an extracurricular literary club and helped launch the annual student literary/arts journal *The Jolie Rouge*. He earned a BA in Spanish (with an English minor) from Indiana University and an MALS (Master of Arts in Liberal Studies) from the University of Southern Indiana.

He has published original fiction and essays as well as translations from Spanish in a number of literary journals in the U.S. and abroad; most recently in issue 16 of JewishFiction.net (translation of story by María Gabriela Mizraje) and in *Rosebud* (honorable mention for essay in the 2015 X. J. Kennedy Prize in Non-Fiction). Also, in Spanish, his essay *"Sobre la reconciliación de contrarios"* appears online in issue 33 of *Letra Urbana*; and another essay, written in English and translated into the common language of Serbia, Bosnia, Montenegro, and Croatia, appears in the premiere issue of *Hourglass Literary Magazine*.

His published books are the YA novella *A Bride Called Freedom* (Ediciones Nuevo Espacio, 2003), a historical romance set in 19th-century Argentina; two translations from the work of Buenos Aires writer María Rosa Lojo: a bilingual edition of her prose poetry collection *Awaiting the Green Morning* (Host Publications, 2008) and the inventive and prize-winning historical-fantasy novel *Passionate Nomads* (Aliform Publishing,

2011); and, most recently, the bilingual edition of Argentine-American author Luis Alberto Ambroggio's tribute to Walt Whitman: *Todos somos Whitman/We Are All Whitman* (Arte Público Press, 2016).

He may be reached via his website at:
www.brettalansanders.wordpress.com
or:
brettalansanders@gmail.com.

www.ingramcontent.com/pod-product-compliance
Lightning Source LLC
Chambersburg PA
CBHW071415090426
42737CB00011B/1466